PUBLIC ADMINISTRATION
Social Change and Adaptive Management

PUBLIC ADMINISTRATION
Social Change and Adaptive Management

N. JOSEPH CAYER and LOUIS F. WESCHLER
Arizona State University

St. Martin's Press   New York

Library of Congress Catalog Card Number: 87-060564
Manufactured in the United States of America.
21098
fedcba

For information, write:
St. Martin's Press, Inc.
175 Fifth Avenue
New York, NY 10010

Cover Design: Ben Santora

ISBN: 0-312-00330-7

To Our Students

PREFACE

Public Administration presents an interpretation of American public administration. Each of the seven chapters is an essay on an interpretive theme that contrasts the demands of rationality with the constraints of real life in public administrative organizations in an uncertain world. To establish the contrast, we examine what is expected of public administration and public administrators and then examine what affects them as they attempt to live up to those expectations. Our use of the swamp metaphor helps to contrast the ordered and neat world of the rational ideal with the uncertain, constantly changing nature of the real world in which public administration occurs.

We hope that our interpretations lead the reader to question critically and examine the reality of public administration. Further, we hope that this book will help the reader develop a personal framework for understanding the complexity of public administration in a changing, unstable environment.

Public administration normally is viewed as application of rational processes to the accomplishment of governmental agency missions. In reality, however, complex forces make rational pursuit of goals difficult. Public agencies and administrators find themselves in the administrative swamp. They are surrounded by competing interests and forces that make administrative life uncertain. This book deals with the reality of public administration and contrasts it to the unreal expectations American society often has of public organizations.

American public administration is practiced in a complex social and political environment. The constraining effects of this environment plus the limits of human rationality lead the practice of public administration to be more fluid than concrete. Public administration and administrators need to be inventive, flexible, and adaptive. Planning, resource allocation, and people management rely more upon intuition and contingency approaches than traditional public administration theory postulates. Public administration is a living experience in which constant personal and organizational adjustments are made as public policy is implemented in a changing and unsure setting.

Additionally, public administration has come to be increasingly important in the general governance of our society. In many respects, the manager is the center of the policy process and, at the service delivery level, is the final decision maker and interpreter of policy. In short, public administrators often determine what the policy actually means.

In attempting to capture the reality of public administration, this book examines the context, major actors, activities, and issues that surround the field. In the first two chapters, we address the context of public administration. Chapter 1 looks at the field of public administration and how people have conceptualized it, with an emphasis on the need for collective human effort to accomplish the objectives of administration. Chapter 2 examines the specific American political context. The effects of political pluralism and the political aspects of administration are used to contrast public administration with administration in general.

Chapters 3 and 4 turn to the organizations and people doing the work of public administration. Chapter 3 focuses on bureaucracy, the dominant form of organization in public administration. Bureaucracy as an ideal, rational form of organization for accomplishing any goal is contrasted to the reality of bureaucratic behavior. Complaints about bureaucracy and suggestions for reform are examined to provide an understanding of the prospects for success. Chapter 4 turns to the individual members of the bureaucracy and what motivates them. Theories of organization, from the perspective of the role of the individual in organizations, are used to illustrate problems in organizational behavior.

Chapter 5 examines the major activities of bureaucracies in carrying out their responsibilities. In particular, we look at the ways bureaucracies use planning, budgeting, and evaluation to facilitate administration. Various approaches to each of these activities and problems associated with *rational* conduct of such activities are considered.

Chapter 6 considers how the problems and activities examined in the previous chapters might be addressed so as to improve public administration. The issues are examined in the context of limited resources and the uncertainty of the environment in which public administration takes place. Recent trends in public administration, which provide both opportunities and restraints for improving practice, are examined as well.

Chapter 7 considers the prospects for public administration and attempts to identify enduring issues in the field. The relationship of "new" concerns to enduring issues is explored.

In writing this book, many individuals have been very helpful. Many have influenced our thoughts and interpretations beyond our abilities to recognize and identify them individually. Some, however, have been of very specific assistance. We owe a special debt to Robert Biller, Executive Vice Provost, University of Southern California, for his earlier formulations on the contrast between the swamp and bedrock in the conduct of public administration. We would especially like to thank Sherry S. Dickerson, Research Associate, and Kirk J. Evans, Research Assistant, Arizona State University, for assistance on details throughout the preparation of the manuscript and for reading and commenting on parts of it. Joann Weschler also provided sound editing advice. Our faculty colleague, Erik Herzik, was very helpful in reviewing and commenting on chapter 5. Discussions with Dalton Lee, Assistant Professor, San Diego State University, helped sharpen some theoretical perspectives. Bernard Ronan, currently with the Arizona State Department of Education, contributed to clarification of our conceptualization of public administration. Cherylene Schick deserves much gratitude for assisting us with her word-processing skills and expertise. Her calm and efficient manner helped greatly in times of panic for us. Eleanor Ferrall, Reference Librarian, deserves special thanks for her always cheerful help in finding material in the Hayden Library at Arizona State University.

Reviewers of the manuscript offered careful and immensely constructive evaluation. Their suggestions and insights improved the book throughout. The reviewers were Elaine Johansen, University of Connecticut; Irene Rubin, Northern Illinois University; John W. Swain, University of Nebraska at Omaha; and Dr. Carter B. Schell, Tulsa Junior College. We are also indebted to the St. Martin's staff who helped make the book a reality. Larry Swanson, political science and public administration editor, was patient and understanding throughout. At the same time, he had the ability to keep us close to schedule. We would also like to thank Michael Weber,

Larry's predecessor, who first encouraged us in this endeavor. Thanks also to Judy Tropea, Beverly Hinton, and Denise Quirk.

While this book would not have been possible without the assistance of those mentioned above, we, of course, are responsible for any shortcomings in it.

N. Joseph Cayer
Mesa, Arizona

Louis F. Weschler
Tempe, Arizona

CONTENTS

PUBLIC ADMINISTRATION
Social Change and Adaptive Management

Chapter 1

PUBLIC ADMINISTRATION

Public administration has been compared to life in the swamp (Biller 1978, 1979; Luthans and Steward 1977) because of the uncertainty faced by it. In the swamp, footing is uncertain, the path is unclear, the terrain keeps shifting, and the alligators are mean and hungry. In such a risky setting, a person is hard-pressed to survive.

Administrators must conduct their activities in an unstable environment. They affect and are affected by changing political power relationships, economic swings, and volatile social issues. Because public administrators are supposed to be accountable to elected officials and the general public, they experience pressures to change. In such an environment, it is difficult to know which path to take, whether one will be on solid ground, or where the mean and hungry alligators are lurking. Administrators are fortunate to maintain the status quo let alone get on with major programmatic goals.

The administrative swamp is inhabited by changing political forces, changing economic conditions, the media spotlight, interest groups, and citizen demands. Additionally, internal forces such as employee concerns, interagency conflict, and bureaucratic routines lie in wait for the manager who attempts to drain the swamp and establish firm ground upon which to work. Because of having to worry about all these alligators in the swamp, public administrators are not able to pursue the goals of the organization with undivided attention. Instead, each of these forces affects the resources available to administrators and how they might utilize those resources. There are also many effects for the dynamics of the public organization itself.

In addition to uncertainty in its environment, public administration is difficult to define because its boundaries are unclear. Government is involved in almost everything people do because it is the ultimate provider of services that keep society together and the final arbiter that ensures the activities of one person are not detrimental to others. As government gets involved, agencies are created with administrators to see that government policy is implemented. In policy implementation, administrators also become policy formulators as they develop expertise in what should be done or what will work best in any given situation. Administrators are in a good position to shape the future development of policy through their recommendations to policy-making bodies. At the same time they make policy by giving meaning to the general policy developed by elected public officials.

Also complicating the scope of public administration is the nongovernmental nonprofit sector. Many such organizations serve the public interest by providing public goods and services similar to governmental services and receive public funding. Operating in the public trust, they are subject to governmentally imposed rules and regulations and operate in the public spotlight. Such organizations include the United Way, Red Cross, and cultural agencies such as museums and symphonies. There are also contract agencies for mental health services as well as hospitals and colleges that serve the public interest. Some public interest groups such as the National League of Cities and Council of State Governments and such professional associations as the International Personnel Management Association and International City Management Association are part of the nonprofit sector. While these organizations are subject to many of the same concerns as governmental agencies, in this book we concentrate on governmental organizations in our examination of public administration.

Both the scope of activity and the variety of substantive content of public administration are wide ranging. It is difficult to develop a clear definition of what public administration encompasses. We face this challenge in attempting to define the nature of public administration.

In order to understand public administration, it is necessary to understand the changing environment and the political relationships among actors in that environment. We must also understand the individuals who make up government organizations and the values that shape their behavior and the behavior of organizations. Superimposed on these issues are efforts to develop rational processes and organizational structures to insure proper implementation of public policy. The issues outlined here are recurring themes throughout the book as we attempt to explain public administration as adaptive management in an ever-changing society.

PUBLIC ADMINISTRATION AS COLLECTIVE HUMAN ENDEAVOR

All administration, including public administration, depends upon the cooperative effort of the individuals who make up the administrative organization. In order to accomplish most objectives, the organization needs to attract members and gain their cooperation. Securing compliance and support of members requires that they interact with and adjust to each other. Therefore, administration is affected by all the complexities of human nature. In public administration, the administrators deal not only with those people who make up the organization but must also work with interested members of the political environment. Included are elected political leaders, citizens, interest groups, and clients of the organization. These elements of the political environment affect the ability of the organization to accomplish its purposes. Along with the internal human interactions, these external elements create an ever-changing setting for public administration.

Internal Dynamics

The ability of organizations to accomplish their objectives is greatly affected by the people within the organization and how they interact. The manager and the employees of the organization may operate on the basis of different needs and expectations; therefore, their behavior may differ (Tullock 1965). An organization's managers usually feel the necessity of pleasing elected public officials and thus attempt to control the activities of employees so as not to alienate those external superiors. Managers are interested in appearing to be as competent as possible to their superiors and in having their departments run as smoothly as possible. Their own careers depend upon how well they are perceived to be doing their jobs; thus, they normally want their subordinates to do their work with a minimum of trouble.

The employee may have other concerns. Among them are earning or collecting a paycheck, pleasing the manager, getting along with others in the organization and getting the job done as efficiently as possible. Ralph Hummel (1987) indicates that bureaucrats represent a culture different from the rest of society because they adapt to a set of norms that permits them to accomplish their tasks without getting fully involved in the human aspects of the work. They operate under guidelines developed by managers or others and accommodate themselves to those guidelines. By accepting the ways of doing things as a requirement of the job, they do not have to deal with justifying their actions by their own values. These characteristics are typical of members of large, complex organizations in the private sector as well as in government.

The bureaucrats' personal values often differ from what is required in their roles or positions. As a result, there may be tension between the requirements of the job and the personal concerns of the employee. If those tensions become too strong, the employee is likely to engage in dysfunctional behavior that is then in conflict with the interests of the organization and higher level management. An extreme example of such a situation might be an employee in a public health agency who has very strong feelings against abortion. If that employee's agency funds family planning clinics or works with clients in all forms of family planning including abortion, it is possible that the employee could make it difficult for those clinics performing or clients seeking abortions. The same conflicts could be felt by an employee with strongly opposite views on the subject having to deal with clinics or clients with opposing views. The effect on the organization may be interference with its ability to get its work done effectively.

Employees have other personal interests and concerns which affect their work activity. Their economic security as well as emotional and psychological well-being affect their performance in the organization. If they perceive managerial directions to be inconsistent with their own self-interests, it is possible that they will act in ways that are dysfunctional to the organization. Managers may attempt to impose control, but conflicts are likely to develop between employees and managers, further diminishing the effectiveness of the organization.

External Factors

Public administrators work in an environment in which they have to respond to a variety of outside forces. Public servants have many superiors who often have differing and even conflicting expectations of the public agency. Elected public officials usually have particular agendas they wish the administrators to pursue. Many of the agendas take the form of public policy adopted by legislative bodies or directives of chief executives. However, many times the newly elected officials expect the administrative agencies to fall in line with their policy preferences even if they are in conflict with formally established policy. The primary concern of many elected public officials appears to be control over the activities of public agencies. In particular, they do not want public administrators to embarrass them or do things that are contrary to their policy preferences. They claim that they were elected to run things.

Problems emerge for public employees when different elected officials desire different behaviors from the agencies. There are always differences based on policy preferences of individual elected officials. Additionally, public agencies often get caught in the middle of conflicts between elected executive officers and legislative bodies. Each may have a different agenda and goal yet the public agency must serve and attempt to satisfy both. In addition to having differing agendas and goals, executive and legislative officials may interpret the same policy in differing ways thus increasing the difficulty for public administrators.

Theoretically, public administrators exist to serve citizens. It is impossible to satisfy the desires of every individual in all ways; thus, some calculation of the "public interest" occurs. This estimation is inexact, does not result from any particular system of rational understanding, and often depends upon impressions. Further, the public interest often is defined outside the agency by elected policy-making bodies, and the administrator must interpret and adjust this abstraction to practice. An important fact for the administrator is that individual citizens expect responsiveness. When they perceive that administrators are not responsive to their needs, they complain. It is not easy for a public servant to explain that the interests of the general public come before those of any one individual. The public administrator is put in the position of attempting to follow agency guidelines and general public policy while satisfying elected officials and individual citizens all at the same time. These are inevitable conflicts which the administrator must juggle.

The public interest often is defined by interest groups that have resources to gain access to administrative agencies. In the absence of a clearly defined public interest, administrators react to those who make claims in the public interest. Interest groups have their own stakes in the activities of agencies. They pressure agencies to interpret and implement policy according to their best interests, again putting public administrators in the position of mediating conflicting demands.

Clients of the organization are most directly affected by the actions of public agencies. Agencies created to serve a particular clientele often are hampered in doing so because laws or administrative regulations limit the flexibility of the administrator to act. The law or regulation may require that families be residents of the state or locality for a specified period of time before they are eligible for services. Thus, a family with no food just arriving in the locality may not be eligible for food assistance. The administrator who has to deny the assistance is perceived as being cold and impersonal. Yet the administrator has little flexibility to change the rule. On the one hand, the policy to provide food represents one value of society, while the rule regarding eligibility represents another. The power to resolve the conflict between the two values may or may not be within the discretion of the public administrator.

These elements of the external environment constrain administrative options and influence agency actions that produce outcomes. Conflicting external signals and expectations lead administrators to act in ways that maximize the ability of the organization to survive. Often they react by attempting to routinize activities in such a way as to insulate themselves from as much pressure as possible. They fall back upon bureaucratic rules and procedures when pressed and pulled into situations that appear to threaten the agency.

PUBLIC ADMINISTRATION AS ART, SCIENCE, AND CRAFT

The nature of public administration has been subject to debate for as long as it has been studied. People argue over whether it is an art, craft, science, profession, field of study, or discipline (Berkley 1985). While there has been a great deal of debate over these issues, there are few definitive agreements or answers to the debates. In reality, public administration is each of these things to some degree although individuals may differ on how they view it. The most long-standing debate has centered around whether public administration is to be considered an art or craft on one hand or a profession or a science on the other.

As Dwight Waldo (1977) indicates, the Scientific Management movement crystallized the debate by attempting to establish public administration as a science with universal laws or tendencies that could be applied in any situation. Humans are viewed as malleable, to be shaped to the needs of the organization. Once the general laws are codified, people may be taught to apply them in any given situation.

Challenges to this approach suggested that management is a practical skill that is based upon highly variable personal characteristics and abilities. These skills and abilities can be acquired and honed through training or may be a part of one's personality. The skills and abilities also vary according to the situation or environment in which they are used.

Experience suggests that many of the accepted principles and practices of Scientific Management do not endure societal changes or transfer to other societies. Therefore, they are suspect as science. Nonetheless, the scientific method can be used in many management situations and can be useful in decision-making processes. Science as a method of inquiry and a body of knowledge may be used to inform managers and estimate the possible consequences of actions. Science, however, is a tool with considerable limits in management. Because management depends upon the coordination of human beings, nothing is totally predictable or certain. Thus, public administration is part of the social sciences which are inexact as measured by the standard of the life or physical sciences. That caveat does not mean that public administration should not strive for as much certainty as possible. Rather, scientific approaches are incorporated as appropriate while public administrators understand that much of their success depends upon adaptation to ever-changing circumstances. Much of their adaptiveness flows from intuition and feelings rather than from facts.

Those who perceive that public administration should aspire to be a science believe that political values can be separated from the administrative process. Values are represented by the policymakers who are separate from the administrators. Thus, the policy/administration or politics/administration dichotomy evolves from the effort to establish public administration as a separate entity. Woodrow Wilson's essay, "The Study of Administration" (1887), gave intellectual legitimacy to the concept of separating politics and administration. This approach to the field has been remarkably durable. While the separation is continually challenged and public administration now eschews the reality of the separation, it is an important analytical distinction for understanding many aspects of public administration. Until the late 1950s and the 1960s, the separation of policy and administration was accepted virtually as a given in the field.

The development of the council-manager form of municipal government, which began in 1908, is perhaps the most dramatic symbol of the policy/administration dichotomy. The plan, which separates the policy function (council) from professional scientific management (manager), has become the overwhelming choice of citizens for city government. Its popularity continues today with well over three-quarters of the cities nationally using the council-manager system. The approach is mirrored in school districts in which boards of education are the policymakers and the superintendent and other professional staff are managers.

In the post–World War II era, scholars began to challenge the purported scientific nature of the Scientific Management School. Herbert Simon (1976) characterized the principles of administration advocated by the Scientific Management School as proverbs that often conflicted with one another or whose opposites were just as plausible. Simon favored attempting to develop a truly scientific approach to administration but also developed a fact-value distinction as a guide to the new science. The fact-value distinction led to a renewed interest in the policy/administration dichotomy. The major impact of Simon's work was to stimulate an interest in more scientific approaches to analyzing public administration. Much of the quantitative study of public administration owes its start to Simon's challenge. Of course, quantification is not synonymous with science although many treat it as such.

As public administration achieved an identity and attempted to utilize the methods of science, it also began to assume some of the characteristics of a profession. The organization of several associations of public administrators such as the International City Manager's (later to be Management) Association in 1914 and the New York

Bureau of Municipal Research (renamed the Institute of Public Administration) in 1906 signaled the legitimacy of public administration as a field of study and practice. Several other associations, particularly the American Society for Public Administration (ASPA) established in 1939, helped to foster a sense of professionalism. As Newland (1984) notes, these events symbolized the maturing of public administration and that the leadership of the emerging field had the prestige to have significant impact on public policy.

As professionalism developed in the field of public administration, new debates over whether it was really a profession also emerged. During the 1940s, a debate raged between Herman Finer (1941) and Carl Friedrich (1940) and their respective followers. Finer saw responsibility in public administration requiring responsiveness to elected officials and adaptation to changing environmental forces. Friedrich took the position that administrators must answer to a scientific standard represented by their expertise and fellowship of science as represented by professional organization standards and accepted practice. The debate over responsiveness and accountability had implications for the "science" vs. "craft" debate about public administration as well as for the development of it as a profession. Those who wish to ascribe strict professional standards to public administration reflect Friedrich's perspective while those who are more concerned with it as a craft and practice are likely to feel more comfortable with the Finer perspective.

The controversy over whether public administration is a profession often devolves to a disagreement on semantics. Frederick Mosher (1968) attempted to address the issue by distinguishing between the established and emerging professions. The established professions would be those such as medicine, which already have a well-ordered system of standards of conduct and a method for enforcing them. The emerging professions, such as personnel management, are in the process of developing appropriate standards and methods of enforcing them. The debate over whether public administration is a profession and how strict the definition must be emerges regularly in the literature (Kline, 1981; Stewart, 1985). There seems to be growing consensus that public administration is a profession in a general sense but that the rigid standards by which many professions are judged are impractical for it. Nonetheless, attempts to establish more conventional professional criteria are made, as in the American Society for Public Administration's 1984 adoption of a code of ethics for public administrators. A major problem with development of such standards is in their implementation. A very small proportion of the people who work in public organizations actually belong to ASPA or other associations. It very well may be impossible to impose codes of conduct on people who do not first accept a specific professional association as the legitimate developer of standards.

Along with development of public administration as a profession, a field of study emerged. Wilson's essay in 1887, in addition to legitimizing the politics/administration dichotomy, has served as a major intellectual beginning for American academic public administration. During the 1930s and 1940s the literature on public administration as an academic field of study burgeoned, and many academics were brought into administrative positions in government. The administration of Franklin D. Roosevelt, in particular, included many of the leading academics in public administration. Leonard White's introductory text first published in 1926 set an agenda for the field of study that was to endure through the early 1960s. Newland (1984) characterizes the 1930s–1950s as the Golden Era of public administration. It was an era of optimism about the impact the field could have on improving government along with a strong sense of community among the scholars and practitioners in the field. Simon's work and the rise of "scientific" political science in the 1950s began to drive a wedge between the academic and practitioner perspective. As with many other parts of society, during the 1960s the sense of community and innocence of the field were severely challenged. The challenge led to a loss of the unity of feeling which had characterized the Golden Era. Today there is much more diversity in the field with numerous areas of specialization that have developed their own professional identities and many ways of approaching the study and profession of public administration.

In addition to the differences about what public administration is, there is a natural conflict between the study and the practice of it. The practice of public administration was firmly established before its identity as a specialized field of study was fully developed. Although a few professional programs of public administration were established in the 1920s, most academic institutions eschewed separate professional studies programs; thus, the field of public administration long existed as a subfield of political science in most colleges and universities. During the 1950s and 1960s, the opposition to professional degree programs in public administration crumbled and programs proliferated. With this proliferation there also came much diversity of research and study. Many practitioners felt that university programs were too theoretical and not relevant to their interests and concerns. During the past twenty years, many efforts to bring practitioner and academic institutions together have been made. The result is a much closer relationship of scholarship to practice, especially in the independent schools and departments of public administration that have more flexibility to reward faculty members for practical work.

RATIONALITY IN PUBLIC ADMINISTRATION

As Morstein Marx (1957) indicates, public bureaucracies are created with a sense of purpose and are expected to apply specified means to accomplish specified objectives. In other words, public agencies are supposed to be rational organizations because they have to get things done as specified by some outside authority under the conditions of the rule of law. To get those things done, methods or means are identified and pursued. The rational approach is virtually a given in the development of organizations.

This form of rationality may be referred to as institutional or procedural rationality and is at the foundation of traditional public administration theory. The ideal of rationality is often not achievable, however, because of numerous forces or conditions under which public sector organizations operate. Foremost among the problems is the fact that most organizations actually have multiple goals, and the goals are often ill defined. Also, as time passes, organizations may be given new goals. The result is that the organization can simultaneously pursue incompatible or conflicting goals. Such behavior is substantively rational. What is rational then depends upon which goal the evaluator expects the organization to pursue. The Nuclear Regulatory Commission, for example, was supposed to regulate nuclear power at the same time it was supposed to promote it. It may not be reasonable to expect that an agency charged with promoting nuclear energy is going to be as critical as it should be in regulating it. Some people would consider the conflicting aims and activities to be irrational. Subunits within the commission pursue the two different major goals. From the perspective of each subunit, it is acting rationally given the goals it has to pursue. What is rational to one subunit may be in conflict with the goal of the other.

Subunits of the organization may diverge in other ways in their pursuit of organizational goals. Subunits develop their own norms and ways of doing things which may or may not be consistent with the needs of the organization as a whole. The resulting dissonance may impede rational pursuit of the overall goal.

Along with conflicting goals, public organizations often find that their rational pursuit of a particular objective may be interrupted by changing goals. New administrations may bring new goals with them, and organizations find that their activities suddenly conflict with the goals of their political superiors. For example, when the Reagan administration came to office, equal employment and affirmative action policies were deemphasized and opposed by the administration. After twenty years of developing rules and regulations and means to implement them, many federal agencies were being asked to abandon their efforts. For state and local governments, which had spent much time and money complying with a growing list of federal government requirements on equal employment and affirmative action, the switch seemed irrational. Changing goals make it difficult for an agency to behave consistently.

Public sector agencies also find that differing publics may interpret their purposes differently. Even members of legislative bodies which create agencies disagree on what an agency should be attempting to accomplish. Interest groups, clientele, citizens, and elected political leaders may also differ on what the agency should be doing and usually attempt to influence the agency. As political power shifts among these competing groups, agency agendas also often shift.

Even assuming that there is agreement on the goals of the organization, there are still many limits to rational action by the agency. Individual rationality often comes into conflict with organizational rationality. Individual employees come to the organization with differing assumptions, norms, and values. Each employee has the potential of having interests that are incompatible with those of the organization. One objective of an organization is to get the employees to temper their incompatible interests and values so as to work in concert with the organization. Given that organizations are made up of many individuals, it is not surprising that many conflicts develop. Employees accommodate the conflicts in many ways, ranging from suppressing their own interests to sabotaging the organization. In the vast majority of cases, individuals are able to reconcile their own needs with those of the organization.

In addition to the conflicts between individual and organizational rationality and among subunits, many other factors affect the capacity of an organization to pursue its ends in a rational manner. Complete rationality requires perfect information, unlimited time, and slack resources. In real life, it is almost impossible to have complete information. Given limits in time and other resources, organizations have to act on the basis of partial information. While the decision or action may be rational in terms of the information available, it is not rational in the comprehensive sense. Especially in the public sector, time may be an important factor. Because of political factors, agencies may make decisions or take actions which they otherwise would not. Even if decisions are made on the basis of complete rationality, there are always some critics who criticize regardless of what is done.

In 1986, the Challenger space shuttle accident in which seven crew members died illustrates the point. There were many charges that NASA went ahead with an unsafe launch despite warnings by engineers that malfunctions would occur if the temperature were below a certain point. Critics of the decision to go ahead charge that NASA was under pressure from the administration and the media for a success. Additionally, it was suggested that NASA was concerned that its forthcoming calendar of launches would be detrimentally affected by another delay. The Challenger was launched with tragic results. If perfect scientific information had been available and used, it is unlikely that the launch would have taken place. Political and time constraints may have affected NASA's willingness to consider all the information. There were other goals besides the launch of the Challenger shuttle that affected the decision-making process. Of course, the money available to collect information is usually inadequate to assure complete information. If agencies wait until all information is available, they are likely to take no action.

While it is assumed that organizations proceed rationally, it is unlikely that they can be expected to be perfectly rational in their actions. With the incredible variety of pressures under which public agencies operate, it is difficult for them to know what they should be doing. Thus, how rational they are is difficult to measure.

GOVERNANCE BY BUREAUCRACY

Modern bureaucracy arose from efforts to make administration more productive, neutral, legal, and rational. Max Weber's ideal construct of bureaucracy (Weber 1968) as the most efficient method of organizing activity conformed to traditional public administration theory and practice. In a positive sense, bureaucracy is viewed as the most rational way of accomplishing any activity and is an inevitable part of our society. Basically, bureaucracy is a form of organization that is hierarchical, impersonal, formal, and based on specialization, rules, and merit. While Weber believed that in its ideal construct, bureaucracy was the most rational and efficient way of organizing, others focus on the dysfunctional and nonrational aspects of bureaucracy (Blau and Meyer, 1971; Argyris, 1960). For example, paying doctors in a public hospital according to the number of patients they see may be dysfunctional to the overall goals of the hospital. Doctors may be inclined to see as many patients as possible and not take as much care as they should in diagnosing problems. The result is likely to be poorer health care than intended. The behavior is dysfunctional to the goal of providing the best possible care. The resulting behavior may be rational from the perspective of the individual doctor's goals but nonrational from the perspective of attaining the goals of the hospital. Weber, himself, had doubts about some of the same issues and utilized the ideal type as an intellectual construct to analyze elements of reality rather than as an accurate description of reality (Weber 1968).

Whether people believe that bureaucracy is the best alternative for organizing or believe that it is dysfunctional, complex modern society is dominated by it. Bureaucracy is a logical result of the positivist reaction to industrial society, which called for expansion of government into virtually all activities of society (Weiss, 1979). While it is popular to denounce bureaucracy as incompetent, inefficient, and too large, people also expect government to perform services for them. Even if they favor reductions in services, they want cuts in services that *other* people use. Governmental bureaucracy is the result of these expectations of government. Individualistic action or choice is impractical for accomplishing the tasks of government.

There is extensive use of bureaucratic organizations in the public sector and bureaucratic government has many implications for self-governance. As Nachmias and Rosenbloom (1980) note, there are inevitable conflicts between bureaucracy and democracy. Democracy presumes plurality and diversity, while bureaucracy requires unity. Dispersion of power and equal access are essential to democracy, while bureaucracy demands a hierarchy of authority. Command and control are integral to bureaucracy, but democracy requires liberty and freedom. Officials of bureaucracy are appointed and enjoy long tenure, while democracy means election of officials with relatively short terms and potentially frequent turnover. In democracy, everyone is to have opportunity to participate in the process whereas in bureaucracy, participation is limited by where one fits in the hierarchy of authority. Finally, democracy cannot exist without openness, while bureaucracy thrives with secrecy and control over information.

These conflicts between democracy and bureaucracy lead to tensions between citizens and public agencies as well as between elected officials and bureaucracies. The tensions often result in the disparaging view people have of government as citizens come to feel that there is little efficacy in participating because they feel helpless in the face of powerful bureaucratic organizations. Nachmias and Rosenbloom (1980) believe that the dominance of bureaucracy and its increasing power give rise to a crisis of legitimacy in United States government because people are discouraged from participating.

Eugene Lewis (1977), on the other hand, believes that bureaucracies have actually displaced legislative and other elected officials as representatives of constituents. Although Lewis is still critical of the effects of bureaucracy, he does suggest that individuals and groups do have access and notes that some groups view specific bureaucracies as their particular representative organizations in government. He uses the example of the Department of Agriculture as an advocate for farmers with various parts of the department representing different farming interests. The same could be said of the Departments of Labor and Commerce. Labor organizations view the Department of Labor as their representative, while the business world looks to the Department of Commerce to represent its interests. Whenever presidents have suggested combining the two departments, each constituent group has reacted negatively.

Although Lewis sees bureaucracy playing the role of representation, he also believes that it makes victims of people. The large and complex bureaucracies in government and society in general do not have time or resources to pay attention to all members of society. Some get lost and become victims by inattention to their problems. The homeless and the hungry are examples of those who suffer from inattention. In many cases, the policymakers have not provided programs for them. In others, agencies have to develop criteria to distribute the limited resources they have. Some people get left out. Others are victims by virtue of the fact that some decisions and actions of bureaucracy have detrimental effects for some individuals. While there may be many beneficiaries of a new freeway system, those who lose their houses to the path of the freeway may not view it as very beneficial. Instead, they may be victims because they lose the only home and security they may have known. Their psychological and emotional security may be irreparably damaged. The need of complex society to act bureaucratically leaves little room for consideration of an individual who does not fit the common denominator.

Bureaucracies supposedly operate to serve the needs of society in general, but they may also be captured by special interests or the self-interest of the individuals who make them up. Vincent Ostrom (1974) notes that individual bureaucrats develop their own missions, especially protection of their own self-interests and thus may lose sight of the purposes for which they are employed in the first place. It is difficult for elected politicians and citizens to maintain control over the missions of bureaucracies. It is also possible that bureaucracies develop alliances with their clientele or those they regulate and then pursue interests benefitting those groups rather than the general public interest. Given that the public interest is difficult to define, it is difficult to control bureaucracy in the public interest. Some even suggest that bureaucracy represents a stable and continuing bias in favor of dominant interests. Greenberg (1974), for example, argues that the positive state represented by big government/big bureaucracy is really based on protection of economically powerful interests. Thus, organized groups—big business, big labor, big agriculture—dominate to the detriment of the interest of individual citizens.

While bureaucracy implies many problems and difficulties for democratic government, it is difficult to imagine government functioning without it. Recognition of its effectiveness leads to its continuing use. Discovery of its negative implications can provide the basis for developing methods of mitigating them. We can be certain that bureaucracy is going to be a part of our modern society for the foreseeable future. Learning to live with it and to harness it to our needs may be our only option.

The next chapter examines the political context in which public administration takes place and the effects of uncertainty and instability in the political environment for rational action.

REFERENCES

Argyris, Chris. 1960. *Understanding Organizational Behavior*. Homewood, Ill.: Dorsey.

Berkley, George E. 1985. *The Craft of Public Administration*, 4th ed. Boston: Allyn & Bacon.

Biller, Robert P. 1978. "Public Policy and Public Administration: Implications for the Future of Cross-Cultural Research and Practice." *Korea Observer*, 9: 253–84.

Biller, Robert P. 1979. "Toward Public Administrations Rather Than an Administration of Publics: Strategies of Accountable Disaggregation to Achieve Human Scale and Efficacy and Live within the Natural Limits of Intelligence and Other Scarce Resources." In *Agenda for Public Administration*, ed. Ross Clayton and William B. Storm, 151–178. Los Angeles: School of Public Administration, University of Southern California.

Blau, Peter, and Marshall Meyer. 1971. *Bureaucracy in Modern Society*, 2d ed. New York: Random House.

Finer, Herman. 1941. "Administrative Responsibility in Democratic Government." *Public Administration Review*, 1: 335–350.

Friedrich, Carl J. 1940. "Public Policy and the Nature of Administrative Responsibility." *Public Policy*, 1:3–24.

Greenberg, Edward S. 1974. *Serving the Few: Corporate Capitalism and the Bias of Government Policy*. New York: Wiley.

Hummel, Ralph T. 1987. *The Bureaucratic Experience*, 3rd ed. New York: St. Martin's Press.

Kline, Elliot H. 1981. "To Be A Professional." *Southern Review of Public Administration* 5: 258–281.

Lewis, Eugene. 1977. *American Politics in a Bureaucratic Age: Citizens, Constituents, Clients and Victims*. Cambridge, Mass.: Winthrop.

Luthans, Fred, and Todd Steward. 1977. "A General Contingency Theory of Management." *Academy of Management Review*, 2: 181–195.

Morstein Marx, Fritz. 1957. *The Administrative State: An Introduction to Bureaucracy*. Chicago: University of Chicago Press.

Mosher, Frederick C. 1968. *Democracy and the Public Service.* New York: Oxford University Press.

Nachmias, David, and David H. Rosenbloom. 1980. *Bureaucratic Government USA.* New York: St. Martin's Press.

Newland, Chester A. 1984. *Public Administration and Community: Realism in the Practice of Ideals.* McLean, Va.: Public Administration Service.

Ostrom, Vincent. 1974. *The Intellectual Crisis in American Public Administration.* rev. ed. University, Ala.: University of Alabama Press.

Simon, Herbert A. 1976. *Administrative Behavior: A Study of Decision-Making Processes in Administrative Organizations.* 3d. ed. New York: The Free Press.

Stewart, Debra W. 1985. "Professionalism vs. Democracy—Friedrich vs. Finer Revisited." *Public Administration Quarterly,* 9: 13–25.

Tullock, Gordon. 1965. *The Politics of Bureaucracy.* Washington, D.C.: Public Affairs Press.

Waldo, Dwight. 1977. "The Prospects of Public Organizations." *The Bureaucrat,* 6: 101–113.

Weber, Max. 1968. *Economy and Society: An Outline of Interpretive Sociology,* eds. Guenther Roth and Claus Wittich; trans. Ephraim Fischoff et al. Vol. 1, ch. 3. New York: Bedminster Press.

Weiss, Carol H. 1979. "Efforts at Bureaucratic Reform." In *Making Bureaucracies Work,* ed. Carol H. Weiss and Allen H. Barton, 7–26. Beverly Hills: Sage.

White, Leonard D. 1926. *Introduction to the Study of Public Administration.* New York: Macmillan.

Wilson, Woodrow. 1887. "The Study of Administration." *Political Science Quarterly,* 2: 197–222.

Chapter 2

THE AMERICAN POLITICAL CONTEXT

The political context of American public administration constantly changes. Political conflict contributes considerably to the uncertain terrain of the administrative swamp. Elected officials, lobbyists, interest groups, and citizens interact in the American pluralist political system in such a way that public administrators often are hard pressed to find the best way to carry out their agencies' missions and at the same time survive in a turbulent political setting.

Public administration is a value-based human endeavor that requires people to act out values within a political context that in itself is value laden. This condition of values within values long has troubled American public administration. A continuing value since the earliest attempts to professionalize public management has been the desire to neutralize administration by reducing its political vulnerability and culpability. Efforts ranging from the passage of civil-service laws to the adoption of professional codes of conduct were used to separate administrators and administration from politicians and politics. Always, commentators have noted that it is not really possible to completely separate administration from politics; nonetheless, this conceptual division has been a continuously guiding ideal of the American administrative tradition.

Democracy makes it especially difficult to develop a politically neutral public service. Much of the political life of a democracy concerns the resolution of value conflicts. Public managers and agencies, as key participants and arenas in democratic processes, must deal with political values. The continuing struggle has been to satisfy the requirements of popular government and value-conflict resolution on the one hand, and the desire for a professional system of public management free of partisanship, on the other.

The concern is rather basic. As Herbert Simon (1976) reminded us some time ago, all human decisions are composed of *factual* (scientifically warranted) and *value* (preference) components. A decision always is a mixture of and a trade off among value and factual aspects of the same issue. Simon's characterization of a fact-value dichotomy has been disputed philosophically, empirically, and practically, but the essence of this characterization remains: decisions are mixtures of objective (factual) and subjective (value) considerations. Simon has a preference for basing decisions as much as possible on factual statements, but he sees that all decision makers are constrained and influenced by a myriad of personal, group, organizational, and societal values. It is useful to remember that one of the basic dilemmas of management is the melding and balancing of the objective and subjective aspects of a given choice situation.

Since values remain forever a part of decision making, it follows that politics, as a system of dealing with values in a democracy, remains an essential part of the context of administration as well as a part of the administrative process itself.

PRIVATE AND PUBLIC IN AMERICAN POLITICS

American government and politics have their roots in liberalism. Anglo-American liberalism developed in the political writings and practices of seventeenth- and eighteenth-century England. We now consider many of its tenets—free market economics, protection of property rights, political individualism, and limited government—as conservative. Yet the political doctrines formulated by such theorists as Thomas Hobbes, Adam Smith, and John Locke were not only radical for their times but laid much of the moral and philosophical foundations of the American experiment with self-government. For better or worse, we are all the children of these believers in secular government, science, humanism, and extreme individualism (Lowi 1969).

There is an inherent tension and contradiction between the liberal notion of limited government and the practice of contemporary bureaucratic government. Although much of the tension is historical, the editorial pages of our daily newspapers and interpretive radio and television news broadcasts amply illustrate the continued debate about the appropriate role of government in the every-day lives of Americans. Public administration is in many ways the stepchild of liberalism. Administrators are asked to do more and more for people as the role of government expands. But they are asked to provide health care, corrections, protective services, welfare, streets, parks, clean water, a more desirable physical setting, better public transit, housing, and education among other things within the context of a political ideology that stresses individual rights and private property above all other goods. Thus, we live a contradiction. We retain our allegiance to the central tenets of liberalism, while at the same time requiring our administrators to implement policies characteristic of the socialist democracies of Europe, such as Sweden, Denmark, and France.

The starting place of most public policy in the United States is the market (Lindblom 1977). Even with the tremendous growth of government since the 1930s, we still have a market-based economy. A majority of goods and services is still provided by private individuals and firms. This economy is underlain by the ethic of capitalism and the tenets of liberalism which stress private ownership of the means of production and an unregulated market in which individual sellers and buyers transact "business." Not withstanding that we live in a more and more regulated economy and society (Hughes 1977; Wilson 1980), we continue to hold firm to the ideology and many of the practices of capitalism.

Conservative and Liberal Interpretations of "Liberalism"

Although we are all liberals to some degree, there is division of opinion about the proper role of government in our society. Some people, usually called "conservatives," favor limited government (Friedman 1962; Kristol 1978; Reich 1983) and other people, now called "liberals," support a more active, positive role for government (Burns 1963; Carnoy and Shearer 1980; Thurow 1980).

Conservatives have more faith in the private market and support policies that promote a free, minimally regulated market system. In their view, market mechanisms, acting out demand and supply equations, have priority over collective actions such as government. The role of government, true to liberal roots and capitalist ethos, is to do those *few* things that the market cannot or will not do. Notwithstanding the fact that these *few* things have become an almost uncountable *many* things, conservatives tend to see government as doing the residual group of activities not done by the individuals and the market.

Government and, by extension, public administration are often *not* seen as essential, primary activities, but rather as supplementary, secondary activities. It is more than mildly ironic that in our post-industrial society, where the public sector heavily regulates private action and provides a vast variety of goods and services, government is so poorly regarded.

The liberal stance is very different. Government is viewed as the friend and defender of ordinary people. The power of the state is to be used as a positive instrument to overcome the limits and biases of the market economy and the maldistribution of income resulting from unchecked capitalism. Individualism and freedom are valued in their own right, but contemporary liberals feel that collective action is required to carry out the ideals of egalitarianism and democracy.

Proponents of a positive role for public authority see government as the ultimate arbiter and protector of those without other resources. The progressive policies of the New Deal and the War on Poverty were based on the idea that governmental power and public administration were necessary instruments in the reorganization and reform of our economy and society. In this view of political life, administrators and agencies are agents of democracy in the push toward social justice.

The debate between the political right and left continues, but more as a variation on a theme than as a fundamental cleavage in our political system. Liberals all, our historic, ideological bias toward individualism and privatism has had a profound effect upon the way we conduct our politics. The fountain of political interaction is *private* want (Arrow 1951; Laver 1981). Individual citizens are expected to express their demands for government action, and governments are expected to respond to these expressions. Notice the direct analogy to the way the market is supposed to work. Citizens, as consumers of publicly provided goods and services, *demand* of the government a certain array of these goods and services. Further, they are willing to *pay* for them through their tax contributions and their participation in politics. Government, in turn, *supplies* the array of goods and services demanded of it. This is a simple model of governance as practiced in America, but it does provide a useful model of how things happen (Wade and Curry 1970; Laver 1981).

Political Pluralism and the Group Theory of Politics

Despite emphasis on individualism and democracy as ideals, the American political system is largely based upon political interaction among associations of individuals rather than individual citizens. Long ago, observers saw that few ordinary citizens have access to the actual working of policymaking (Lasswell and Lerner 1952). Instead, they saw a system in which the demand function is dominated by interest groups and lobbyists. These observations led to the development of the "Group Theory" of American politics.

As propagated by Arthur F. Bentley (1908), David Truman (1951), Earl Latham (1952), E. E. Schattschneider (1960), and Robert Dahl (1966), this theory of interactive political groups became the standard interpretation of how American politics works. Known as "pluralist democratic theory," this body of normative and interpretive thought, conceptually derived from James Madison's *Federalist 10* (Hamilton, Madison, and Jay 1961), and much of it based on empirical political science of the 1950s and 1960s, postulates that the building blocks of American politics are interest groups. These interest groups are coalitions of persons sharing common values and wants organized for the expressed purpose of demanding that governments perform specific acts for the members of that group. These are *private* associations whose main purpose is the lobbying of government to secure their own *private* ends (Edelman 1964; Key 1967).

In this model, government officials are "brokers" and "producers." Governments, the *public* arenas in which interest groups play out their private demands, permit officials to broker among the various interests to achieve some sort of compromise and trade-off among competing interests. Note that this puts government and especially the legislative function in a passive, though central, stance and role. The legislature and legislators receive and respond to demands made upon them by lobbyists representing interest groups. The initiative is in the hands of the interest groups.

Over time, interest groups have come to be known as "pressure groups." They put pressure on elected and appointed officials to get what they want. By the 1980s, various kinds of pressure groups, often acting through political action committees (PACs) had come to dominate most of the demand function of political communication and to provide major resources to the electoral and legislative processes. PACs are organizations developed by pressure groups to provide support for or opposition to specific candidates for public office. The PACs permit these groups to put large amounts of money into electoral campaigns and to avoid many of the restraints of state and federal campaign control laws.

Thus, we have come to have a kind of a democracy in which politically active groups rather than individual citizens are the key units of expression. Some commentators doubt that lobbyists and PACs actually represent the values of the members of the larger associations they claim to represent (Schattschneider 1960; Rose 1967; Parenti 1970). This appears to make little difference as decision makers act as if these agents do in fact represent the "public" or "publics" they claim to. The pluralism in this theory is an artifact of the existence of many groups competing for attention. In any given arena, for any given issue, and at a given time, there may be several lobbyists and advocates seeking to get their message across to the governmental brokers.

A few moments' reflection about this group-based explanation of American politics suggests that it is flawed and masks some very important issues in our representative democracy. First, not all citizens and interests are evenly represented or even represented at all. There is a bias to this pressure-group system that overrepresents the interests of the business community and the owners of capital wealth (Connolly 1969). Second, the degree of competition among groups may be more apparent than real. Stable coalitions of interests and logrolling are not uncommon in the operation of interest groups (Riker 1962; Buchanan and Tullock 1962). Third, administrative agencies often act as interest groups in their own right which often produces a conflict of interest between their *public* function of implementing policy and their *private* function of getting their fair share of the budget (Borchering 1977).

THE IRON TRIANGLE

Pressure-group politics has led to the fusion of interest groups, legislative committees, and administrative agencies into stable alliances, which may be characterized as "Iron Triangles" (Cater 1964;

Heclo 1978). These Iron Triangles are the natural consequence of pressure-group politics in which agencies strive to develop their own political space and leverage.

It is well-known that Congress's major work is done in committees and subcommittees. Lobbyists spend considerable time cultivating both the legislative members of these committees and their staffs. Agencies and subagency components likewise specialize in subject matter and in linkages with legislative committees. Members of Congress and their staffs in turn demand and make use of the specialized information and knowledge of lobbyists and agencies. Thus, there are literally hundreds of the tight little semi-closed systems of communication among legislative-interest group-agency actors. They are interdependent, functional fiefdoms (Harrigan 1981).

There are triangles within the triangles, as illustrated in Figure 2.1. The outer shell of this polygon is the triangle composed of the interest group, the legislative committee, and the agency. The person representing each of these units might be the head lobbyist of the pressure group, a key member of the legislative committee, and the head of the agency. Inside of this outer grouping is a more intimate, functionally more specialized, tighter triangle composed

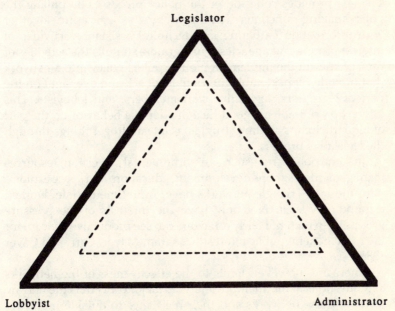

FIGURE 2.1: Iron Triangle

of a member of the committee staff, a member of the lobby staff, and a middle-level member of the agency management. This inner group is likely to make up the continuous operational network of the triangle.

The interaction of the competent parts of the Iron Triangle provides integration of the policy process. Considerable day-to-day communication takes place among the members of the inner shell of the triangle. Middle-level managers, legislative staff personnel, and lobby staff members frequently meet to discuss common concerns. Equally important, they produce much of the information used in the legislative process and provide technical support both to individual legislators and to legislative committees. Finally, they are likely to be the persons who actually set up hearings and agendas for hearings.

There is also much communication among the members of the outside shell of the triangle but perhaps not as continuous and sustained as that in the inner shell. Together, this communication binds the participants together very tightly and does much to overcome some of the barriers set up by our constitutional system of separation of powers and checks and balances. In a sense, the Iron Triangle provides cohesion in the policy processes by pulling the policy-making functions dominated by the legislature together with information gathering and technical assistance activities of interest groups and agencies. Furthermore, it pulls the activities of the agencies in the implementation of public policy into a network that provides considerable informal feedback and oversight on the part of legislators, legislative staff members, and lobbyists. This interaction promotes a good deal of adaptive behavior on the part of all participants as they struggle as a team to get things through the legislative process.

In some policy areas such as environmental protection, resources management, weapons development, education, and space exploration, the Iron Triangle networks have, from time to time, worked astoundingly well. Not only have the interests of the pressure groups been met, but fairly often one can see productive concern for the more general public interest (Cochran, Mayer, Carr, and Cayer 1986).

There are, however, limits to the effectiveness of the networks and questions about their propriety. A major concern is the narrow focus of these networks and their resistance to outside input. As highly specialized, functionally defined policy fiefdoms, the alliances of interests, legislatures, and agencies tend to be closed off and inaccessible to other values. This fragments policy and reduces the overall effectiveness of governmental efforts. Further, the Iron Triangles tend to protect established values, status quo groups, and established power relationships. They resist change and encourage incrementalism in both policy and the budget process. Finally, they shield what could and should be public processes from public and media scrutiny. Sunshine laws requiring public exposure notwithstanding, the Iron Triangles encourage covertness in government, not a healthy condition in a democracy.

ADMINISTRATORS AND AGENCIES IN POLITICS

Administrators often act as lobbyists and agencies as pressure groups (Rourke 1976). Notable in this regard have been the U.S. Army Corps of Engineers, the Department of State, the Federal Bureau of Investigation, the Park Service, the National Aeronautics and Space Administration, and the Environmental Protection Agency. Yet, administrative politics goes far beyond the role of advocacy in the legislative process. To a considerable extent administrators are coming to be the key linkages in the broader political processes of American government.

As key actors in politics, especially in policymaking as opposed to electoral politics, agencies may be seen as elitist organizations in their own right or as extensions of the general political elite. Some inquiry about the political role and function of bureaucracy suggests, to the contrary, that administrators and agencies are steadily becoming *more* representative of their constituents than are most legislative bodies (Lewis 1977). This observation begs the question of how generally representative of the public American government actually is, but it does suggest that as the public sector has become the major employer in the nation, administrators are the *most* representative class of "rulers." Access and representation via bureaucracy is especially important to groups generally underrepresented in government—women and racial and ethnic minorities.

In spite of the considerable efforts of reformers to depoliticize administration and of practitioners to professionalize management, it is not trite to remark that for better or worse, public management is in the middle of politics. To an extent unanticipated by founders of the good government and professionalization movements at the turn of this century, managers have become central actors in the morality plays we call the political processes.

Listing what administrators *may not* do politically is easier than listing what they *actually* do in politics. In most jurisdictions, laws and professional codes of conduct specifically restrain most public administrators from actively engaging in partisan electoral politics. They may vote and belong to political parties, but they may not openly personally endorse candidates for elective office nor use their position or public funds to support candidates. Further, they are circumscribed in the use of their public positions and public funds for lobbying purposes.

Nonetheless, even these limits are eroding. Public employees often form collective bargaining units, associations, and groups which in turn have PACs that actively engage in partisan politics. Further, many if not most local governments, state agencies, and federal bureaucracies conduct lobbying in the interest of promoting and protecting that organization's interests in the policy processes, especially in budget making. Even more sophisticated political networking and communication frequently takes place as administrators and agencies develop and provide support for policies and legislation and use their considerable expertise to shape the course of public policy. An interesting example is municipal police. Considerable effort was expended between the 1920s and the 1970s in reducing corruption, developing well-trained, professional police forces, and removing the police function from direct political influence. The net result has been the development of highly proficient, professional state and local public safety systems throughout the nation. All this effort toward reform, development, and professionalization has not, however, removed police administration from politics (Wilson 1968).

In most areas, we are past the days of massive corruption and favoritism. But in some ways, this has simply changed the quality of the political communication. Successful police chiefs and departments are fully aware of the political functions of management. The police department, as in the case of all city departments, must engage in political communication and bargaining to do its job well.

Public administrators and agencies have come to play a variety of important political roles and functions. First, as noted in the discussion of the Iron Triangle, top and middle managers are often in the position of advocating in policy-making processes to gain resources for their agencies and programs. They must go to the mayor, city manager, governor, council, or legislature to promote policy recommendations, oppose undesirable legislation or policies, and protect budget shares.

In a sense, civil servants are the only full-time lobbyists. They are continually defending their turf. Such advocacy is so much a part of their jobs that we often make such non-bureaucratic activities a key part of the job description and expectation of top managers. Can you imagine a municipality hiring a police chief or a doctor to head a public health department who lacked the skills to advocate well for their city departments and to promote the city government in the larger community?

Second, managers frequently cultivate outside support for their agencies. Most agencies provide specific services to distinctive users or relate to specific persons or organizations in the larger society. Departments of fish and game, flood control agencies, educational institutions, police departments, and regulatory commissions all have target groups which often become "clientele" or support groups. The agency works hard to meet the goals of this group and the group works hard to support the agency and its personnel in the mass media, legislative process, and the central administration. Obviously not all administrative functions and agencies, foreign aid and prisons as examples, lend themselves well to the development of clientele relationships, but those that do energetically promote this two-way dependency and those that do not have the natural opportunity to develop such a relationship try hard to develop substitutes such as cultivation of friendly members in legislative staffs, support from good government organizations, and mutual support pacts with comparable agencies in other parts and levels of government.

Third, agencies and agency personnel are very frequently the targets of media campaigns, lobbying activities, and direct citizen inputs. At all levels, we are experiencing the repoliticalization of the public bureaucracy. Most managers can testify to the hail of daily phone calls, visits, and requests aimed at them, many of which deal with political as compared to the technical or administrative aspects of policy.

The street-level administrator—teacher, police officer, garbage collector, post deliverer, game warden, and employment clerk—not only receives most of the complaints and the hard looks, but also often receives much of the political pressure from user groups, media, and elected officials. The street level tends to cope as well as it can and pass as much of the political pressure up as possible (Lipsky 1976).

Managers and administrators at all levels find themselves in the midst of political communication with the outside world. It is axiomatic that top management bears most of the political pressure and most of the political communication. Yet, it often is the middle management level that provides the political continuity of the agency. Remember the earlier metaphor of the Iron Triangle. The middle manager is in the midst of a lateral set of relationships which tie the organization on a day-to-day basis with the other actors in the policy process. Although there is little empirical work on the role of middle management in external political communication, case and anecdotal materials support the idea that middle managers perform much if not most of the day-to-day external politics as well as the internal politics of an organization. Top management tends to deal with the larger goal setting issues and with political emergencies. The mudane, "who do we see about this," political communication is the meat of the middle manager. Thus, the concept of the "manager in the middle" states well the idea of the middle manager caught in the middle of day-to-day politics of organizations.

THE CHANGING ENVIRONMENT OF PUBLIC ADMINISTRATION

The environment in which administrators play political roles is changing at an ever-increasing pace. Who would have predicted in 1960 that Ronald Reagan would be elected president in twenty years, that we would have major urban insurrections, that we would have an antiwar movement, that environmental concerns would be a part of everyday life, and that half of the work force would be women? In 1970, few people thought our economy would be so unstable, energy so expensive, local government so strapped for resources, and agriculture in such poor shape. By

1980, we were more used to rapid change, but now we face PACs, the neo-Christian movement, higher levels of local participation unheard of ten years before, rapid turnover of elected and appointed officials, and metropolitan regions larger than any one can imagine. Further, futurists must continually revise their predictions and trend forecasts to keep up with history.

Administrators increasingly face an unstable environment. In the face of such complexity, ambiguity, and rapid change, conventional methods of coping are not very useful. Public managers more and more must rely on a combination of strategic planning and contingency management to adapt to the unsure conditions they face.

The observation that public administration takes place in an unsure setting is not new. At least since the 1920s commentators have stressed the rapid change in the roles of our government and our nonprofit organizations, and the corresponding changes of setting in which public management takes place (Ogburn 1922; White 1926). Such factors as rapid urbanization, the rise in international power of the United States, and resource development in the western states provided a heady, changing environment for public management during the early decades of this century. Several wars and depressions later, a vastly more urbanized society and an internationalized economy present public managers with an even more unsure environment. The current environment is vastly different from that of the past, but public administrators have had to wrestle with rapid, complex change since the beginning of the movement toward a professional public service in the late 1890s and early 1900s.

American public administration was born in confidence at the turn of this century. Many persons believed that given training in appropriate principles of management, sufficient resources, and proper setting of community goals, there was little that governmental administrators could not accomplish. In our current ethos of mistrust of government and politics, this optimism seems both misplaced and unrealistic. Nonetheless, the high expectations of founders such as Frank Goodnow, Woodrow Wilson, and Luther Gulick helped forge a profession in which few saw serious limits to the application of human intelligence and ingenuity to the management of organizations for solving social problems.

We have learned much about the limits of public administration since then. We have had enormous successes in the development of the national park system, irrigation of the arid West, recovery from the Great Depression, waging of World War II, development of nuclear energy, provision of the interstate highway system, and space exploration, among other important national programs. These successes pale considerably when considering the more limited successes and failures of the war on poverty, development of more secure weapons systems, provision of health care for the impoverished and the aged, reduction of crime, reform of the justice system, equal treatment of citizens, affirmative action, provision of homes for the homeless and street people, redistribution of income, tax reform, and environmental protection. We continue to discover that technology, human skills, natural resources systems, organizational capacity, economic resources, and political systems all have limits. Further, the number, range, and complexity of social problems increase faster than our capacity to deal quickly with them. As we have tried what we thought were good solutions, such as Head Start, Revenue Sharing, Urban Development Grants, and Auto Emissions Testing Programs, we become impressed with the limits of our capacity to reduce poverty, increase education, revitalize our cities, and reduce air pollution. All these programs are more expensive, less effective, and more problematical than we at first thought. They all have been qualified successes in some respects, but none have done the full job expected of them.

The plain fact is that our political environment is so complex and interconnected and our knowledge base so limited that it is a testimony to human skill and ingenuity that social programs work as well as they do. We live in an age of avowed risk and uncertainty rather than in the age of perceived certainty of our ancestors.

LIFE IN THE ADMINISTRATIVE SWAMP

Problems and goals are not as clear as they once seemed. On a national level, we continue to struggle with the main direction and goals of our governments, but there is little agreement and not much prospect of agreement in the near future. At the community level there often is more agreement on goals, but not about how to reach them or about who shall provide the resources to pay for the solutions. Organizations and managers in the past have thrived on firmly fixed goals. The prospects for this kind of firm guidance are not good. We find communities seriously examining in considerable depth such basic questions as what is social equity, can we afford current ranges of public services, and do we want big government.

Traditional management practices not only require the setting of goals, but they depend upon the development of good, usable knowledge and information bases. Knowledge is continually expanded. It is well-known that we live in the age of information, but it is not as clear that we have the applied knowledge we need to design effective organizations, select optimizing solutions, and monitor program implementation to see if things are working out well. Our recent experience in dealing with social issues suggests that we do indeed lack fundamental understanding of how our policy options may or may not work.

Public agencies find more often than not that they lack sufficient economic and human resources to meet their mandated and expected service levels. Cutback management, reduction in force, cost savings, and service reductions are all too familiar to public officials, especially those in local governments. Under these conditions, public managers face a double bind. There is less and less tolerance of error and fewer resources available to use in recovery from error. The probability of error, selection of the wrong solution or practice, increases in the face of high risk or uncertainty.

In this book, we characterize this generally unsure, rapidly changing environment of public management as "life in the administrative swamp." Administrators frequently do not know the best path through the murky, unsafe surroundings. Danger abounds and there are few reliable clues to guide one to safety. They may well select the wrong path and sink into the marsh or be eaten by alligators. Sink or swim has a much too real meaning in these uncertain days.

What can a reasonable, professionally dedicated manager do when faced with the swamp? Change the basic approach to problem solving. Managers are well on their way toward the development of a new way of management based upon dealing with uncertainty and limited resources. American public administration is entering a new era in which managers are becoming more and more sensitive to their political environments and are trying to develop flexible approaches with multiple ways of reaching solutions to the problems thrust upon them by a more active public.

Along with the changing political context in which they operate, public agencies and managers are faced with alligators from within. In the following chapter, we examine the culture of bureaucratic organizations. This culture, characteristic of many governmental agencies, is as problematic and threatening as the rapidly changing external setting.

REFERENCES

Arrow, Kenneth. 1951. *Social Choice and Individual Values*. New York: Wiley.

Bentley, Arthur F. 1908. *The Process of Government*. Evanston, Ill.: Principia Press.

Benveniste, Guy. 1981. *Regulation and Planning: The Case of Environmental Politics*. San Francisco: Boyd and Fraser.

Borchering, Thomas. ed. 1977. *Budgets and Bureaucracy: The Source of Governmental Growth*. Durham, N.C.: Duke University Press.

Buchanan, James, and Gordon Tullock. 1962. *The Calculus of Consent*. Ann Arbor, Mich.: University of Michigan.

Burns, James MacGregor. 1963. *The Deadlock of Democracy*. Englewood Cliffs, N.J.: Prentice-Hall.

Carnoy, Martin, and Derek Shearer. 1980. *Economic Democracy: The Challenge of the 1980s*. White Plains, N.Y.: Sharpe.

Cater, Douglas. 1964. *Power in Washington*. New York: Vintage.

Cochran, C. E., L. C. Mayer, T. R. Carr, and N. J. Cayer. 1986. *American Public Policy: An Introduction*. 2d ed. New York: St. Martin's Press.

Connolly, William E., ed. 1969. *The Bias of Pluralism*. New York: Atherton.

Dahl, Robert. 1966. *Pluralist Democracy in America*. Chicago: Rand McNally.

Edelman, Murray. 1964. *The Symbolic Uses of Politics*. Chicago: University of Chicago Press.

Friedman, Milton. 1962. *Capitalism and Freedom*. Chicago: University of Chicago Press.

Hamilton, Alexander, James Madison, and John Jay. 1961. *The Federalist Papers*. New York: New American Library.

Harrigan, John J. 1981. *Political Change in the Metropolis*. 2d ed. Boston: Little, Brown.

Heclo, Hugh. 1978. "Issue Networks and the Executive Establishment." In *The New Political System*, ed. Anthony King, 87–124. Washington, D.C.: American Enterprise Institute.

Hughes, Jonathan R. T. 1977. *The Governmental Habit*. New York: Basic Books.

Key, V. O., Jr. 1967. *Politics, Parties and Pressure Groups*. New York: Crowell.

Kristol, Irving. 1978. *Two Cheers for Capitalism*. New York: Basic Books.

Lasswell, Harold, and Lerner, Daniel. 1952. *The Comparative Study of Elites.* Palo Alto, Calif.: Stanford University Press.

Latham, Earl. 1952. *The Group Basis of Politics.* Ithaca, N.Y.: Cornell University Press.

Laver, Michael, 1981. *The Politics of Private Desires.* Middlesex, England: Penguin.

Lewis, Eugene. 1977. *American Politics in a Bureaucratic Age: Citizens, Constituents, Clients and Victims.* Cambridge, Mass.: Winthrop.

Lindblom, Charles E. 1959. "The Science of Muddling Through." *Public Administration Review,* 19: 79–88.

Lindblom, Charles E. 1977. *Politics and Markets: The World's Political and Economic Systems.* New York: Basic Books.

Lipsky, Michael. 1976. "Toward a Theory of Street Level Bureaucracy," In *Theoretical Perspectives on Urban Politics,* ed. W. D. Hawley. Englewood Cliffs, N.J.: Prentice Hall.

Lowi, Theodore. 1969. *The End of Liberalism.* 2d. ed. New York: Norton.

Ogburn, William F. 1922. *Social Change.* New York: Viking Press.

Parenti, Michael. 1970. "Pluralism: A View from the Bottom," *Journal of Politics.* 32: 501–530.

Reich, Robert B. 1983. *The Next American Frontier.* New York: Times Books.

Riker, William. 1962. *The Theory of Political Coalitions.* New Haven: Yale University Press.

Rose, Arnold. 1967. *The Power Structure.* New York: Oxford University Press.

Rourke, Francis E. 1976. *Bureaucracy, Politics and Public Policy.* 2d ed. Boston: Little, Brown.

Schattschneider, E. E. 1960. *The Semi-Sovereign People: A Realist's View of Democracy.* New York: Holt.

Simon, Herbert A. 1976. *Administrative Behavior: A Study of Decision-Making Processes in Administrative Organizations,* 3d. ed. New York: The Free Press.

Thurow, Lester. 1980. *The Zero-Sum Society.* New York: Basic Books.

Truman, David B. 1951. *The Governmental Process.* New York: Knopf.

Wade, Larry L., and Robert L. Curry. 1970. *A Logic of Public Policy: Aspects of Political Economy.* Belmont, Calif.: Wadsworth.

White, Leonard D. 1926. *Introduction to the Study of Public Administration.* New York: Macmillan.

Wilson, James Q. 1968. *Varieties of Police Behavior.* Cambridge: Harvard University Press.

Wilson, James Q. ed. 1980. *The Politics of Regulation.* New York: Basic Books.

Chapter 3

BUREAUCRACY: PROMISE, PATHOLOGY, AND REFORM

Public policies are administered by public organizations, the dominant form of which is bureaucracy. Public bureaucracies are expected to accomplish their tasks effectively and in a way that is responsive to the desires of the public or elected officials representing the public. While this objective seems very simple on the surface, it is subject to a widely varying definition. The end result is that agreement on effectiveness and responsiveness is difficult to achieve. Lack of agreement on their meanings allows bureaucracies discretion concerning the way they carry out and assess their activities. With discretion, there is the potential for abuse.

THE PROMISE OF BUREAUCRACY

Bureaucracy is the antithesis of the swamp in that bureaucracy's purpose is to develop order and make things predictable. By creating rational order and procedures for the accomplishment of organizational goals, bureaucracy attempts to ferret out the alligators in the swamp, shed light on the darkness, and plan for dealing with the rising water. The promise of bureaucracy is that it is rational, objective, and thorough, thus implying predicability and consistency in application of authority (Weber 1968). That bureaucracy has difficulty in living up to its promise leaves it open to a great deal of criticism.

Bureaucracy, in its ideal form as portrayed by Weber, is based on a hierarchical system of authority where roles, rules, and regulations are the basis for actions. Decisions regarding personnel are based on merit suggesting that expertise, knowledge, and performance are the major criteria for evaluation of employees. Additionally, employees work full time for pay rather than having a property right to their positions, and neutrality is the hallmark of the system. Specialization of task is also an important component—it allows the greatest efficiency in performance of individual tasks. The hierarchy of authority is the coordinating mechanism that brings all the specialized activity together in pursuit of the common goal.

The Weberian model was consistent with developments in government and business in the United States in the late nineteenth century. The development of large industrial concerns led to many bureaucratic organizations in business. In the public sector, the civil-service reform movement which had its beginnings in the early part of the century came to fruition in the passage of the Pendleton Civil Service Act of 1883. The Act incorporated many of the concepts found in Weber's ideal construct of bureaucracy, especially neutrality and an emphasis on merit in personnel processes. These approaches were affirmed by Woodrow Wilson's essay "The Study of Administration" (1887).

During the Golden Era of Public Administration (the 1930s to 1950s) (Newland 1984b), the intellectual traditions of the field were firmly established and they took their cues from the likes of Wilson, Gulick and Urwick (1937), Leonard White (1926), and Weber. The field of public administration grew with a focus on the structure of the organizations utilized to administer policies. The separation of politics and administration or policy and administration was accepted as given and appeared in the titles of major books in the early development of the field. Bureaucracy developed with an emphasis on separation of the administrative process from the policy-making process and from partisan political activities. This development was especially true at the national government level. It was not until the 1920s and after that most state and local governments witnessed widespread reform efforts aimed at making administration neutral. During the middle part of the twentieth century, state and local governments came more and more under the reform influence. While there are still unreformed governments, the principles associated with Weberian bureaucracy are almost universal in government in the United States. Through mandates from the national government and through initiatives of their own, state and local units share some of the features of the bureaucratic form of organization.

Bureaucracy is viewed by many as the superior form of organization for handling complex policies and issues. Despite the conservatism of the 1980s, people continue to demand ever-expanding services from government, resulting in growth of the state and bureaucracy which implies greater control over the activities of individuals. People then become concerned about the loss of liberty and want a reduction in government activity. Because individuals normally want a reduction in activities other than those that benefit them, there is little agreement on how the size of the state can be reduced. Also because so many people have a stake in maintaining each activity or program, reduction is difficult to accomplish. The result is that bureaucracy has grown to the point where it is seen by some as the dominant force in our political system.

BUREAUCRATIC PATHOLOGY

While the characteristics of bureaucracy described by Weber are supposed to lead to efficiency, predictability, objectivity, thoroughness, consistency, and rationality (Argyriades, 1982), those characteristics also affect the ways in which members of the bureaucracy behave. Their behavior can be functional or dysfunctional and may serve the interests of one part of the organization at the expense of another or to the detriment of the organization as a whole. The behavior in which survival of the bureaucracy and protection of its members displace the goals for which the organization was established has been referred to as bureaupathic behavior (Merton 1940; Thompson 1961).

The hierarchical nature of bureaucracy and formal authority represent efforts to control activities of members in the organization. The purpose of such control, of course, is to ensure that the efforts of all members are coordinated toward the goals of the organization. While some control is necessary, there is a tendency to demand complete conformity in many bureaucratic organizations. The tendency toward conformity is a very powerful one that is reinforced by the rewards management has to dispense. Kanter (1977), for example, found that success in the organization was highly dependent upon effective team membership represented largely by conformity to the team's norms.

Other key forces that support conformity are the socialization processes of the organization, the desire to belong, self-interest, peer pressure, and lack of self-confidence. On the negative side, fear of punishment such as loss of the job and security are also important to many members of the organization. Each of these factors affects individual members differently, but there is little disagreement that the pressures to conform are strong and present in most organizations, especially large, bureaucratic organizations.

Although conformity is important to the coordination of efforts within the organization, it can have negative effects if carried too far. The culture which develops in bureaucracies leads to situations in which members operate only within the sphere of authority they perceive themselves to have. Thus, they look for specific authorization to do anything. Such a preoccupation with formal authority often means that the bureaucrat is internally responsible but is able to avoid external accountability for actions. The bureaucrat can decline to act because of lack of authority or can hide behind performing a very narrow action that is not sufficient to deal with the problem at hand but that satisfies his or her need to operate within legitimate authority. To the frustrated citizen who is shuffled from one desk or office to another, the issue of getting action is probably much more important than who has the authority to accomplish the task.

Conformity can also be dysfunctional to the organization as a whole because it is strongest in the most homogeneous subunits of the organization. Thus, the further down the hierarchy of the organization one goes, the greater the sense of group norms is likely to be. The conformity within the small subunit may be such that members of the subunit actually resist the authority that is supposed to be the coordinating force within the organization. The subunit may become so cohesive that it strives to become insulated from the organization as a whole.

Along with the hierarchical structure of bureaucracy, specialization of activity can be detrimental. Specialization is conducive to the work of the organization to the extent that it fosters the application of the greatest expertise to any given part of the work of the organization. By concentrating on their particular activity, bureaucrats can develop great proficiency in what they are doing and organizational efficiency can be enhanced. On the negative side, however, is the fact that they can use that narrow expertise as a way of resisting control by those in higher level positions. The expertise can be used as leverage in dealing with other parts of the organization. Because others are unlikely to have full knowledge of the area of activity of a specialized subunit, it is difficult for others to make judgments about recommendations or requests of those subunits.

As specialized functions develop, professional standards and norms also develop around those activities. The professional standards and norms cloak the specialists with a sense of neutral competence, which contributes to greater credibility with the rest of the organization and the external environment. This credibility can be used in resisting control from those outside the particular unit.

Efficiency of operation in a particular activity may be enhanced by specialization, but highly specialized units may lose sight of the overall goals of policies and objectives of the organization. By focusing on the specialized activity, bureaucrats may exaggerate the importance of their activities and lose sight of how they relate to the rest of the bureaucracy and policy process. They can often concentrate on their own activity, which may inhibit the ability of the organization as a whole to function properly. The specialized activity may become the real goal to the bureaucrat in that activity.

The concentration on specialized activity may also lead to a loss in communication across subunits of the organization with the result that there is little cross-fertilization of ideas. With the loss of new perspectives, the organization may stagnate and become less effective. Too little openness to what is going on in other subunits or too little interaction with others reduces the variety of ideas and inputs to organizational activities. Further, it reduces the possibility of using horizontal communication networks to coordinate activities among different units or agencies, all of which have some part of the action in implementation of a given policy.

Specialization can result in isolation from outside ideas which, in turn, often leads to a phenomenon known as "groupthink" in which group norms are so strong that realistic appraisal of a situation is difficult or impossible. Irving Janis (1972) studied decisions regarding such situations as the Bay of Pigs, Pearl Harbor, the invasion of North Korea, and the expansion of the effort in Vietnam and found that United States decision makers were severely hampered by groupthink. He found that the groups dealing with each of these situations became so close-knit that they developed norms that caused them to avoid negative feedback and to develop mechanisms to keep such feedback from the leader. Additionally, warning signals were ignored, and information that disagreed with their norms was reasoned away. Members of the groups tended to screen their own input, and critics were dismissed as not understanding the situation. The members lost the ability to identify with the concerns of those outside the group. Acceptance of the group viewpoint became paramount.

Clearly, such a situation does not contribute to the most rational decision-making process for government. The experiences in these situations are repeated every day in organizations. The Watergate scandal of the Nixon administration and the scandal over Iranian arms deals in the Reagan administration represent the us-against-them mentality which is symbolized by groupthink. On a much smaller scale, decision making in subunits of bureaucracy reflects similar characteristics. Such tendencies do not contribute to effective decision making or public service.

Rules, regulations, and procedures have a tendency to become more important than the goals of many organizations. This phenomenon is referred to as goal displacement, because abiding by the rules and regulations becomes the goal or takes precedence over doing what the rules were created to accomplish. Rules may ease the work of the bureaucrat and provide predictability to the activities of the organization. For the client wishing to be served, however, rules may get in the way of effective service. The question arises as to whether the organization exists for provision of service or for protection of the bureaucrats. Obviously, there is much room between these two extremes. It is also certain that some people become so frustrated by the rules they have to follow that they give up and never receive the service. In some instances, however, the client has little choice. If individuals wish to drive an automobile, they have to put up with the rules and regulations of the state and local licensing bureau. Stories and complaints about those offices are legend, yet little seems to change in them.

In order to be fair and equitable in dealing with the public, bureaucracies are expected to practice impartiality and neutrality. Once again, a noble objective often results in a less than desirable effect. Neutrality and impartiality can be carried to the extreme so that bureaucracy becomes impersonal. Equality of treatment may lead to an inappropriate remedy for a specific situation, and the bureaucrat is viewed as unresponsive. While bureaucrats may hide behind the rules as a way of avoiding doing something, they frequently have no power to mitigate the effects of the rule.

Bureaucracies develop personalities of their own. Often the norms of the bureaucracy are self-protective in nature and border on the pathological (Merton 1940; Thompson 1961). Such norms and behaviors help bureaucrats defend themselves from others such as superiors, political leaders, clientele, and the general public. Some of the activities explained in the discussion above play a role in such protective behavior. Additionally, bureaucrats develop a language of their own commonly called "bureaucratese." Bureaucratese allows members of the organization to communicate with each other in more precise terms, but it also allows bureaucrats to better control the situation when dealing with outsiders. Ralph Hummel (1987) claims that bureaucratese's primary function ". . . is to make outsiders powerless." Whether that is the main purpose or not, the effect of jargon is to intimidate those who have to deal with the agency because they do not have the advantage of knowing the language. Academic disciplines experience the same situation with development of language specific to their fields. Remember the first time you encountered terminology in academic public administration. Language serves to build a cohesive organization, but it may impede effective delivery of service if clientele cannot understand what is required of them or what is available to them.

Many students of bureaucracy have identified several common tendencies in bureaucratic behavior (Downs 1967; Merton 1940; Schon 1971; Thompson 1961). Generally, it is concluded that bureaucracies have conserving tendencies. They attempt to hold on to what is comfortable and known, and resist efforts to change things. In protecting their turfs, they tend to develop routines and procedures that serve their interests and limit the ability of outsiders to influence tbeir activities. They are effective at resisting control and have perfected strategies for survival (Greenberg 1974; Kaufman 1976).

While bureaucracies are very effective in socializing members to their norms, there are always some people who cannot conform because of the incompatibility of their own values with those of the organization. These individuals may withdraw from the organization, try to change the organization, or rationalize their activity within the organization on the basis that it permits them to earn the money to do what they really value doing outside the organization. In extreme cases, of course, individuals may attempt to sabotage the organization.

Informal organizations develop within formal organizations as one major way for members to cope with the demands made on them by the formal structure. Classical organization theorists and early pioneers in public administration believed informal organizations to be a negative force. They felt that informal organization should be discouraged and that effective management would prevent its development (Gulick and Urwick 1937; Blau 1963). The Hawthorne Studies led to reassessment and the management literature began to consider the functional effects of informal organizations (Barnard 1938; Mayo 1933). These issues will be addressed more fully in the next chapter.

POPULAR CRITICISMS OF BUREAUCRACY

While bureaucracy is a positive instrument for the implementation of governmental policies and programs, popular sentiment about bureaucracy is largely negative. As Allen Barton notes, popular complaints about bureaucracy focus on three major issues: (1) personal traits of bureaucrats, (2) the structure of bureaucracy, and the (3) relationship of the bureaucracy to the larger political system (Barton 1980).

Personal Traits

Bureaucrats are often characterized as being uncaring and interested only in following rules and regulations because when an individual case does not fit into the rules or regulations, the bureaucrat often sees no way of handling it. To the individual seeking service, the bureaucrat seems insensitive and rigid. Red tape is usually blamed for such lack of responsiveness to the individual case. Bureaucrats often are viewed as people who cannot make it in the private sector and are thus less competent than their private sector counterparts. Similarly, they frequently are considered less motivated than others and overly rigid. Citizens often complain that bureaucrats seem less interested in serving the public than in controlling it and in serving their own interests. While these views are largely inaccurate, they are very commonly held among the general populace. One bad experience with a bureaucrat or agency is rapidly generalized into an indictment of the bureaucracy generally. The hard, effective work of the vast majority of public employees is not readily visible or recognized.

Structural Aspects

Some structural constraints placed upon bureaucracy limit its effectiveness and lead to popular criticism of it. Public policy often imposes specific restrictions on bureaucrats to prevent them from abusing their power. Bureaucrats are permitted to operate only on the basis of specific authority. Dealing with an unusual situation thus becomes difficult. There are restrictions on political activity of public administrators, and personnel rules and regulations are very protective of the individual public employee. Thus, managers often feel frustrated in attempting to make employees responsive because they have limited authority to discipline and especially to dismiss employees. Employee protections in the form of formal hearings and due process are much more common in the public sector than in the private sector.

The concept of employment at will, common in the private sector, is not operative in public employment to any great extent. Employment at will means that the employer can dismiss an employee at any time for most any reason. In the public sector, employees normally can be terminated only for cause. In recent years, laws and court decisions have limited the employment at will doctrine in the private sector, but there are still major differences between the two sectors.

A common view is that the budgeting system tends to work against accountability by rewarding those agencies that spend their money regardless of what they accomplish through its expenditure. Saving money while performing the expected job often is rewarded with budget cuts, while those who spend all they are appropriated and ask for more have justification for greater revenues. There are few incentives for efficiency and many for expansion of activities. Through expansion, bureaucratic managers have larger domains to control and thus greater power, usually accompanied by a larger salary to reflect the greater responsibility. Program evaluation and sunset reviews (in which agencies are automatically reviewed at the end of specified time periods to determine the need for their continued existence) are examples of efforts to control these activities. Political and clientele support for programs and agencies, however, can make these efforts difficult.

The expertise of the agencies and their control over information also is seen as leading to concentration of power by bureaucracies. Through its use of information, bureaucracy has the upper hand in many policy-making decisions even at the expense of the legislative body which is supposed to be the policy-making apparatus. Similarly, the chief executive frequently is powerless to do much to influence the course of events in particular agencies.

As areas of expertise develop, professionalization of the bureaucracy also grows. Professionalization implies the application of knowledge and expertise in ways consistent with standards and codes developed by fellow professionals. These standards and codes are beneficial to the public to the extent that they insure proper and ethical behavior. However, professional groups may also help to insulate the member bureaucrat from external control. The association may attempt to dominate the decision-making process or may claim the allegiance of the bureaucrat. Loyalty to the agency or to the public may be weakened, thus further limiting accountability.

The bureaucrat combines expertise with professionalism and the power of the state to form a "formidable source of power" (Lewis 1977). Cloaked with this power, bureaucrats can be very intimidating to citizens and clientele. Professionalism also gives the aura of neutrality and competence which are important ingredients in dealing with those outside the agency. Professionals often use this image of professionalism and neutrality to attempt to influence decisions outside their areas of competence, especially in decisions about distribution of resources (Lewis 1977).

Political Relationships

The relationship of the bureaucracy to the larger political system provides another area for criticism. Because the bureaucracy is the one permanent institution in the executive branch, it enjoys a certain degree of autonomy. Elected executives and their appointees serve fixed terms and come and go. The bureaucrats in the protected service stay on indefinitely. As a result, they have contacts and support which insulate them from newly elected officials (Pfiffner 1987). The bureaucrat has many tools to make it difficult for the elected official, including interpretation of policy and slow action.

External groups align with bureaucracy to provide another source of support. In particular, clientele of bureaucracies often become major supporters of it. The alliance between bureaucracy and interest groups is viewed by many as a major problem in that it causes the bureaucracy to react to special interests rather than in the general public interest. Despite the fact that it is difficult to define the public interest, the administrative system does tend to favor those interests that are very well mobilized and have the resources to participate in the system. As a result, many concerns may be ignored because those with the concerns have no opportunity to voice them.

The Iron Triangle of interest groups, bureaucracy, and legislative committees reinforces the tendency to react to special interests. Legislative committees depend upon bureaucratic agencies for much of their information and assistance in the policy-making process. Alliances usually develop between particular committees and agencies. Affected interest groups usually maintain close ties with agencies and legislative committees and the three elements work together in mutual support. For example, agriculture committees of Congress, the Department of Agriculture, and large agriculture corporations usually work with one another and understand one another's needs. They realize that if they work together they can accommodate part of each participant's needs. Whether the result is conducive to the general public interest may not be a very high priority. In Fritschler's terms, these alliances are subgovernments in which the bureaucracy, interest groups, and congressional committees come together to fend off forces detrimental to their common interests (Fritschler 1975).

The electoral system also encourages this coalition of interests. While it is theoretically possible for the voters to exert control through elections, incumbents have overwhelming advantage over their challengers in the United States. As incumbents, they have visibility rarely available to challengers and the interests with which they work normally try to keep doors open through contributions to the campaign. Similarly, bureaucracies can be very helpful in providing important information or in the timing of announcements of programs. The incumbent supportive of a particular agency can usually count on some assistance. The result is that the bureaucracy may respond more to the interests of the incumbents or supporters of the incumbents than to the interests of the citizenry at large.

Bureaucrats also have an advantage over other political participants because many of the activities in which they are engaged never become major issues debated in the public arena (Lewis 1977). Thus, they are able to work on particular issues or agendas over concerted periods of time without much public spotlight. Public spotlight on issues tends to change after short periods of time as people get tired of an issue or as new issues gain public attention. The bureaucrat is able to focus and continue interest long after the general public and elected official may have forgotten about an issue. The bureaucrat thus dominates the policy-making process on many such issues. Bureaucratic tenure and the lack of public exposure also have positive effects. They ensure stability of the system and provide continuity of policy and service through times of political change.

While criticisms of bureaucracy are very common and imply dysfunctional effects, some of the items noted may also be functional. As Gerald Caiden (1981) indicates, there is a culture of public organizations which involves adherence to laws, rules, and regulations. The public service is based on the belief that bureaucracy serves the people and is expected to uphold the very highest levels of integrity while operating on the basis of merit and performance. These values, and others, form what Caiden calls the "ideology of public service." Implied in the criticisms people have of the bureaucracy is the expectation that public servants should behave in concert with the very values Caiden has outlined. The criticism stems from the perception that bureaucrats have not lived up to the standards the public has for them.

Despite the bleak picture painted by the criticisms, there are those who believe that the bureaucracy is misrepresented by the critics. While the supporters of the bureaucracy accept the fact that some individuals abuse their positions, they present a picture of a hard-working and ethical public service. Their concern is with how the work of the bureaucracy can be facilitated along with protections from abuse by the few who do not live up to the promise of bureaucracy (Mainzer 1973; Newland 1984a, 1987; Rosen 1978).

REFORM

Reorganization and bureaucratic reform are major preoccupations of many people interested in public administration and policy. Harold Seidman and Robert Gilmour open their influential book (1986) with the statement, "Reorganization has become almost a religion in Washington." Reorganization and reform abound at the state and local level as well. As soon as any problem is identified with any governmental program, policy, or agency, there are advocates of ways to fix the problem through reform. Of course, much of the early development of American public administration was characterized by reform movements. The personnel reform efforts of the late nineteenth century and the local government (good government) reforms of the early twentieth century are good examples of that era. The main objective of reform during this era was to insure neutral competence of public officials.

Reform efforts through the 1920s, 1930s, and 1940s tended to focus on centralizing executive leadership, authority, and responsibility in agencies and in levels of government. The 1921 Act creating the Bureau of the Budget was one of the significant examples of this focus. By the 1950s, the centralizing trend had been very successful in focusing responsibility in departmental headquarters in national agencies as well as many state and local levels. In addition, the national government began the process of centralizing political authority in the national level through public policies that required state and local units to comply with national rules if they were to share in funding of those activities by the national government. Among the most celebrated events accomplishing such an effect was the passage of the Social Security Act of 1935 and its programs. During the 1950s, however, there was an attempt to reverse some of the centralizing tendencies, and the focus became one of attempting to disperse authority (Rourke 1976). The pendulum continues to swing back and forth depending upon the political philosophy of those in office. During the 1960s there was a resurgence of the centralizing tendency followed by the decentralizing emphasis in the 1970s until the present. Similar shifts can be found in different degrees at the local and state levels.

Reform Objectives

Most calls for reform suggest that there is a need to make bureaucracy more responsive to the elected political leaders and the general public (Garnett 1987). In every election, there are advocates of making government responsive and accountable, usually meaning that the bureaucracy has to be brought under control. The assumptions supporting such efforts are that government bureaucrats are serving their own interests or are overly responsive to special interests, both of which are detrimental to the public good (Greenberg 1974; Weiss 1980). Reform proposals often focus on reducing the size and cost of government programs and agencies.

Reform has been pursued with a moral fervor in the United States. The personnel reforms of the nineteenth century were couched in terms of getting rid of the evil of spoils and replacing it with the virtue of merit. The good government movements of the 1920s and afterward had the same good versus evil character to them. Machine politics was viewed as corrupt and in need of dismantling. Administrative reform built upon principles of management and separation of partisan politics from administration assumed a major status in public affairs. Many of the principles are embedded in the early classics of American public administration (Gulick and Urwick 1937). Perhaps the most influential public document in public administration history, the Hoover Commission report (The Commission on Organization of the Executive Branch of Government 1949), emphasized these principles and values.

The political party machines were replaced by a bureaucratic machine. While merit systems and reformed cities abound, bureaucracies dominate the political decision-making process. The interests of the bureaucracies, especially of the middle class who make it up, supplanted the interests of the political parties and their followers (Lowi 1967). The New Public Administration and equal employment/affirmative action policies so important to the 1970s were, in part, reactions to the bureaucratic machine. Reforming the bureaucracy is viewed as a way of returning power to the citizenry.

Reform and reorganization efforts are justified on many other grounds. Especially popular are promises that the reform or reorganization will lead to greater economy, efficiency, and improvement in ability of government to deliver services. As Wildavsky (1961) notes, these kinds of justification for reform often mask political agendas. Reform and reorganization usually have profound effects on the distribution of political power or who gets what in the political system. Thus, many reform efforts are supported by those who hope to benefit directly by the change.

Bureaucratic reform also is supported because it is expected to solve substantive problems of all kinds (Seidman and Gilmour 1986). These justifications are usually linked to improving the ability of the organization to operate more efficiently, thus improving its chances of doing its job. Thus, the military establishment is reorganized every once in a while to reduce waste and corruption but also because it is expected that reorganization will improve defense capability.

The promises made by reformers and proponents of reorganization are often unrealistic. When the expected results do not come, people become frustrated, and the bureaucracy slips even further in its negative image.

Approaches to Reform

Bureaucratic reform occurs in many ways, but there are two fundamental approaches. Reform either attempts to restructure the bureaucratic organization or attempts to change the procedures through which the bureaucracy operates. Most efforts combine elements of both approaches, but usually a reform proposal will fit primarily into one or the other category.

Structural reform is prevalent throughout the history of our political system. The very development of our governmental system relied upon structural features that were expected to limit the ability of government to infringe on the liberty of its citizens. The Constitution spells out structures which many now consider inefficient and outmoded; thus, there are always suggestions for changes that would allow one branch of government or the other to operate with fewer hindrances. Of course, presidents usually want the executive branch unshackled and leaders in Congress usually want greater freedom for Congress. Even members of the Supreme Court call for changes that would speed up the judicial process. These structural elements were placed in the Constitution so that no one branch would be able to operate entirely on its own. Separation of powers and the attendant checks and balances were intended to slow things down and to permit careful consideration of any anticipated action.

Public administration in the United States was built largely on reform of government structure as a way of increasing efficiency and responsiveness of the executive branch of government. The personnel reforms of the ninteenth century were based on separating administrative systems from the partisan political environment. Separation of politics and administration or policy and administration was the major theme of much of the reform movement. While many of the advocates of good government and more efficient government administration during the 1920s, 1930s, and 1940s placed much emphasis on management practices, they also held separation of politics and administration as a sacred tenet.

One of the major features of structural reform is reflected in personnel systems. They are constantly targets of reform. At the national level, in 1883, the personnel system was made semi-autonomous through the creation of the civil service system. While it took many years to develop fully, this civil service system was set up so that it could not be controlled entirely by the chief executive. The same type of development took place at the state and local levels with some actually preceding the national government in development of independent civil service and/or merit systems. Reformers theorized that government would become more efficient and less responsive to particular interests (political machines) with independent personnel systems. As pointed out earlier, the bureaucracies that have developed have their own agendas and respond to particular interests; so, they may be characterized as machines. Those with access to the bureaucracy reap the spoils. Clearly, personnel reform also involves procedural changes which will be addressed below.

By the 1970s, many leaders were calling for structural change in personnel management once again. With the leadership of President Carter, the Civil Service Reform Act of 1978 was passed restructuring the personnel function in national government. Many structural changes took place, chief among them being the division of the U.S. Civil Service Commission into three major units: the Office of Personnel Management, the Merit Systems Protection Board, and the Federal Labor Relations Authority. The effect of the change was to bring the personnel function more closely under the control of the president once again with the Office of Personnel Management being integrated into the executive management function. Now there are calls for change once again as there is evidence of politicization of the personnel function. The same experiences, in varying degrees, are found at the state and local levels. After the national government reform, many state and local units followed suit.

In virtually every agency of government, no matter what level, there are reorganization plans developed on a recurring basis. Some are implemented, others remain plans. It is almost axiomatic that a newly elected president, governor, or mayor will have major plans for restructuring government to make it more efficient, effective, and responsive to say nothing of cutting waste of taxpayer money. The high hopes are often dashed by the reality of having to work with the bureaucracy which has power of its own (Brown 1977).

A highly visible area of structural change is seen in the way the presidents organize their own offices and staffs. In 1921, the Bureau of the Budget was created with responsibility for coordinating the budget process. In 1939, it was moved into the Executive Office of the President reflecting increasing consolidation of presidential control over the budgeting function. In 1970, the Bureau of the Budget was renamed the Office of Management and Budget to reflect changes in its major responsibilities over time. Exactly what the office does and how influential it is depends upon how much the president takes the advice and counsel of the Office of Management and Budget. In each administration, there are differences in which members of the cabinet or Executive Office of the White House have access to, and thus, influence with the president. For example, there is always speculation over whether the National Security Advisor, the Secretary of State, or Secretary of Defense are more important in foreign policy. In each administration, the situation is different in part because of the way the president's office is structured.

Another structural issue popular today revolves around whether government should contract with the private sector to perform many functions, thus eliminating many government agencies and changing the structure of service delivery (Carroll 1987). Contracting for weapons development is a prime example at the national level. In the West, many state and local governments contract with the private sector for fire, sanitation, and water services. Of course, contracting with the private sector for building of highways and other major facilities is common as well. In recent years, there have been many proposals for contracting with the private sector for jails and prisons and other corrections services. The trend to privatization has been very strong in the 1970s and 1980s. Again, this reform is usually justified as facilitating more efficient delivery of services although there is much disagreement about the legitimacy of such a claim.

Procedural reform is also very common. Proponents usually argue that if procedures could be improved, government services could be delivered more efficiently and effectively at great savings in cost. The budget process is a very popular area for reform efforts (Caiden 1987). During the 1960s and 1970s, each new national administration seemed to have a new budgeting system that was going to revolutionize the federal budgeting and management process. We went through program budgeting, planning programming budgeting system (PPBS), strategic budgeting, zero based budgeting (ZBB), and other variations. Each strategy had attractive features to those who wanted to improve government services, but each has been short lived given the strong routines that inhere in the bureaucracy and the Congress. While the new systems might have been used by the administration in its decision-making processes, they usually have had little impact on how the bureaucracy and Congress proceed.

Management and decision making are areas in which reform is constant. Elements of a great variety of decision-making approaches are evident in government agencies. There have been management by objectives (MBO), strategic planning, flow charting, program evaluation and review technique (PERT), cost-benefit analysis and many others. Most techniques are advocated in the interests of making better-informed decisions, thus being more effective in managing in the public interest. Disagreements often develop over who is advantaged by a particular approach.

Evaluation of government agencies and programs has also been a popular cause with reformers. The zero based budgeting system implemented by President Carter built in an evaluation process that was supposed to force units to examine themselves thoroughly in the budget development process.

Related to ZBB is sunset legislation. At the state level, sunset legislation became popular in the 1970s. The objective was to assure that government agencies do not continue to exist once their goals are accomplished. Thus, agencies and programs are created with a specific lifespan, or all agencies and programs are reviewed on a cycle such as every five years. If the reviewing authority (sometimes a legislative committee, sometimes a specially established commission) finds that continuation of the agency or program is not justified, it recommends its abolition. It is not clear how well such systems work. So far, very few programs and agencies have gone out of business as the result of sunset review. Many critics claim that controversial programs are likely to suffer most by the process and that those with powerful interests supporting them have little to worry about.

During the early part of this century, much of the effort in procedural reform focused on attempting to insure that individuals were assured their procedural rights before bureaucracies. Many procedural guarantees developed in regulatory agency activities and court cases regarding their procedures (Davis 1975). Finally, in 1946, the national government passed the Administrative Procedures Act which codified procedural rules required of administrative agencies. Other rules may be found in legislation authorizing programs and agencies. State and local governments followed the lead of the national government and there is now a strong body of procedural protections for anyone dealing with a government agency. Of course, the activism of the courts during the 1960s and early 1970s added to and strengthened those procedural protections (Rosenbloom 1987).

Arising from the procedural protections are the open government and sunshine laws. All levels of government have policies that require open meetings, open records, and access to government information. The Freedom of Information Act of 1966 at the national level is one of the primary vehicles for opening government to the average citizen. While the Reagan administration, like others before it, has been attempting to make access to government information more difficult to obtain, individuals have access to the courts to force release of information. The assumption behind the act is that taxpayers support the development of the information and thus have a right to it. More importantly, the act is built on the belief that control over the bureaucracy and government, essential to democracy, is impossible without information about what the government is doing. State governments generally followed the lead of the national government on freedom of information. Again, the courts have been helpful in extending the right.

Along with freedom of information policies, open meeting laws have given public access to the decision-making processes of governments. Open meeting laws generally dictate that a governing body can discuss or make policy only in a meeting open to the public. There are some exceptions such as for personnel decisions, law suits, and purchase of land. Otherwise, an agenda for the meeting must be publicly posted some prescribed time in advance. The idea is to allow the public to be a part of the decision-making process and make sure that the decision makers are not making decisions without consideration of public input. Such policies also allow the public to be informed about just what is happening and who is advocating what.

Obstacles to Bureaucratic Reform

Reform of bureaucracy is viewed from different perspectives. Advocates of bureaucratic reform view it as the solution to particular problems. Bureaucrats, who are likely to be affected most directly, usually are understandably less enthusiastic about prospects of reform. As Siedentopf (1982) states ". . . structural innovation underestimates administrative conservatism, bureaucratic inertia, and human resistance to change." Bureaucrats and their agencies often feel threatened by the changes others wish to make. When bureaucrats are involved in the development of change, they are more likely to be supportive. However, when reform movements come from outsiders who are critical of the bureaucracy in the first place, bureaucrats are likely to be less supportive of the change.

Bureaucratic Resistance to Change. There are many benefits of stability, and social systems may be viewed as striving to maintain equilibrium (Kaufman 1971; Schon 1971). The bureaucratic routines, standard operating procedures, and the like are strong impediments to change (Smith 1976; Thompson 1969). People in the bureaucracy feel comfortable with the way things have been done, thus making it difficult for them to see how change would improve operations and why they should disrupt their comfortable routine. This reaction is just human nature and occurs in any type of situation.

Because of the specialization of units in the bureaucracy, the bureaucrats may become narrow in their perceptions of what is important. They may view activity in their own units as most important and not be concerned about effects on the organization as a whole. Seeing that their units are functioning well may make them difficult to convince of the need to change since they do not have a good understanding of the rest of the system. They are also likely to have close ties with clientele and others outside the organization who support them in resisting change because of fear of the effects for them. Ties to legislative committees or other supportive forces may be disrupted by change, and the uncertainty is not easily overcome.

There are many costs in changes which affect the ability of the bureaucracy to accept them. There are the sunk costs which arise from previous investment of money, time, and effort. Once resources are committed, no one likes to see them wasted. Because of the sunk costs, every effort is made to see results; therefore, anything that might interfere with perceived payoffs may be resisted. When an organization puts resources into a particular system of operation, it is not likely to abandon that system easily just because someone else has another idea. The psychological costs are also very important. Commitment of individuals to an approach or value system is not easy to change.

There are costs in terms of power as well. The political stakes of managers, employees, clientele, and others affected by the organization and its activities are usually very important considerations. These actors in the process are expected to protect their interests. If they have influence in the organization in the first place, it is likely that they have influenced the structure and processes in such a way as to facilitate their interests. It is not logical to believe that they would give up that kind of influence without resistance. Reorganizations often shift power and influence over organizations and programs.

While many reorganization and reform ideas may be popular, the resources to accomplish them may be very limited. Thus, another obstacle to change is the resource base from which the governmental agency is operating. Of course, resources may be adversely affected by change and thus would lead to resistance.

Overcoming Resistance to Change. Resistance to change is strong, but there are also ways to reduce the resistance. Perhaps the most important strategy to increase acceptance is involving those affected by change in the process of developing the reform. By being involved in the decision-making process, they are more likely to endorse it. If change is imposed from the outside, there is a tendency of the organization members to rally round their organization. If change is internally developed, however, they have an opportunity to structure and influence it and may be supportive of greater change.

Acceptance of change depends upon clear understanding of the change and its implications. If the bureaucrat understands the change and is convinced that it will be in his or her self-interest, acceptance is likely to be enhanced. Similarly, if the bureaucrat's perceptions of the goals of the organization are consistent with the desired change, acceptance is more likely. Finally, the consequences of not accepting the change usually have an impact. A strong-handed approach, however, can also backfire.

PROSPECTS FOR BUREAUCRACY

Bureaucracies are dynamic organizations which permeate our governmental system. While they have features that facilitate their ability to accomplish the purposes of government, they also have features that inhibit their effectiveness and especially their responsiveness to elected leaders and the general public. As a result, continual emphasis on reforming the bureaucratic system permeates political discussion. As political power and ideology shift, they bring pressure for change in government and bureaucracy. As long as the political pendulum continues to swing, so will desire for change.

Carol Weiss (1980) suggests that there are several contemporary trends that will keep bureaucratic reform on the public policy agenda. Declining public confidence is an important factor. Public institutions have suffered greatly in image during the past couple of decades. Scandals in government agencies and, especially in the presidential office, leave people wondering if any public institution can be trusted. The reaction is to try to find ways to reform government to insure against such abuse.

Economic stringency and taxpayer resistance are interrelated phenomena which also affect desire for change. As the economic system struggles, especially relative to foreign trade and the rising national debt, there is a lot of support for reform to lighten the burden of government. The same applies at the local and state levels. Taxpayers have not been inclined during the past fifteen to twenty years to see government revenues increase. Instead, they have been calling for cutbacks in government activity. Reform is seen as one way of decreasing government activity and expense.

The size, complexity, and uncertainty of governmental programs and agencies are also important factors leading to questions about governmental efforts. Because it is not always possible to come up with clear-cut solutions to problems, people become frustrated with public institutions. Many problems are just unresolvable in the strict sense of the word and can be dealt with only as efforts at mitigation. People socialized (as most Americans are) to believe that any problem is capable of solution find it difficult to believe, for example, that we cannot easily solve the drug problem or poverty. When efforts do not pay off in ridding society of the problem, people become impatient and want reform. Bureaucratic duplication and overlap are often blamed as partly responsible for the lack of solutions.

The fragmentation of political parties and proliferation of single-issue interest groups are two other interrelated forces Weiss believes foster efforts for bureaucratic reform. Because political parties cannot really bring people together under specific integrating values any longer, they have difficulty generating continued support for any one approach to dealing with public policy issues. Single-issue interest groups have entered the fray with their focused efforts to influence public policy. Those efforts often include reform of programs and agencies to better achieve their objectives.

There is no doubt that reform efforts will continue to be part of public policy debate. What the result of those efforts will be is much more difficult to predict. Chapter four continues this discussion with emphasis on the individual member and changing forms of organization.

REFERENCES

Argyriades, Demetrios. 1982. "Reconsidering Bureaucracy as Ideology." In *Strategies in Administrative Reform*, eds. Gerald E. Caiden and Heinrich Siedentopf, 39–57. Lexington, Mass.: Lexington Books.

Barnard, Chester I. 1938. *The Functions of the Executive*. Cambridge: Harvard University Press.

Barton, Allen H. 1980. "A Diagnosis of Bureaucratic Maladies." In *Making Bureaucracies Work*, ed. Carol H. Weiss and Allen H. Barton, 27–36. Beverly Hills: Sage.

Blau, Peter. 1963. *The Dynamics of Bureaucracy: A Study of Interpersonal Rela-*

tionships in Two Government Agencies, 2nd ed. Chicago: University of Chicago Press.

Brown, David S. 1977. " 'Reforming' the Bureaucracy: Some Suggestions for the New President." *Public Administration Review*, 37: 163–169.

Caiden, Gerald E. 1981. "Ethics in the Public Service." *Public Personnel Management*, 10: 146–152.

Caiden, Naomi. 1987. "Paradox, Ambiguity, and Enigma: The Strange Case of the Executive Budget and the United States Constitution." *Public Administration Review*, 47: 84–92.

Carroll, James D. 1987. "Public Administration in the Third Century of the Constitution: Supply-Side Management, Privatization, or Public Investment." *Public Administration Review*, 47: 106–112.

The Commission on Organization of the Executive Branch of the Government. 1949. *General Management of the Executive Branch, A Report to the Congress*. Washington, D.C.: U.S. Government Printing Office.

Davis, Kenneth Culp. 1975. *Administrative Law and Government*. St. Paul: West.

Downs, Anthony. 1967. *Inside Bureaucracy*. Boston: Little, Brown.

Fritschler, A. Lee. 1975. *Smoking and Politics*. 2d ed. Englewood Cliffs, N.J.: Prentice-Hall.

Garnett, James L. 1987. "Operationalizing the Constitution Via Administrative Reorganization: Oilcans, Trends, and Proverbs." *Public Administration Review*, 47: 35–44.

Greenberg, Edward S. 1974. *Serving the Few: Corporate Capitalism and the Bias of Government Policy*. New York: Wiley.

Gulick, Luther, and Lyndall Urwick, eds. 1937. *Papers on the Science of Administration*. New York: Institute of Public Administration.

Hummel, Ralph P. 1987. *The Bureaucratic Experience*, 3rd ed. New York: St. Martin's Press.

Janis, Irving. 1972. *Victims of Groupthink*. New York: Houghton Mifflin.

Kanter, Rosabeth Moss. 1977. *Men and Women of the Corporation*. New York: Basic Books.

Kaufman, Herbert. 1971. *The Limits of Organizational Change*. University, Ala.: University of Alabama Press.

Kaufman, Herbert. 1976. *Are Government Organizations Immortal?* Washington, D. C.: The Brookings Institution.

Lewis, Eugene. 1977. *American Politics in a Bureaucratic Age: Citizens, Constituents, Clients and Victims*. Cambridge, Mass.: Winthrop.

Lowi, Theodore J. 1967. "Machine Politics—Old and New." *The Public Interest*, 9: 83–92.

Mainzer, Lewis C. 1973. *Political Bureaucracy*. Glenview, Ill.: Scott, Foresman.

Mayo, Elton. 1933. *The Human Problems of an Industrial Civilization*. New York: Macmillan.

Merton, Robert K. 1940. "Bureaucratic Structure and Personality." *Social Forces*, 18: 560–568.

Newland, Chester A. 1984a. "Crucial Issues for Public Personnel Professionals." *Public Personnel Management*, 13: 15–46.

Newland, Chester A. 1984b. *Public Administration and Community: Realism in the Practice of Ideals*. McLean, Va.: Public Administration Service.

Newland, Chester A. 1987. "Public Executives: Imperium, Sacerdotium, Collegium? Bicentennial Leadership Challenges." *Public Administration Review*, 47: 45–56.

Pfiffner, James P. 1987. "Political Appointees and Career Executives: The Democracy-Bureaucracy Nexus in the Third Century." *Public Administration Review*, 47: 57–65.

Rosen, Bernard. 1978. "Merit and the President's Plan for Changing the Civil Service System." *Public Administration Review*, 38: 301–304.

Rosenbloom, David H. 1987. "Public Administrators and the Judiciary: The 'New Partnership.' " *Public Administration Review*, 47: 75–83.

Rourke, Francis. E. 1976. *Bureaucracy, Politics, and Public Policy*. 2d ed. Boston: Little, Brown.

Schon, Donald. 1971. *Beyond the Stable State*. New York: Norton.

Seidman, Harold and Robert Gilmour. 1986. *Politics, Position, & Power: From the Positive to the Regulatory State*. 4th ed. New York: Oxford University Press.

Siedentopf, Heinrich. 1982. "Introduction: Government Performance and Administrative Reform." In *Strategies In Administrative Reform*, eds. Gerald E. Caiden and Heinrich Siedentopf, *ix–xv*. Lexington, Mass.: Lexington Books.

Smith, Michael P. 1976. "Barriers to Organizational Democracy in Public Administration." *Administration and Society*, 18: 275–317.

Thompson, Victor. 1969. *Bureaucracy and Innovation*. University, Ala.: University of Alabama Press.

Thompson, Victor. 1961. *Modern Organization*. New York: Knopf.

Weber, Max. 1968. *Economy and Society: An Outline of Interpretive Sociology*, eds. Guenther Roth and Claus Wittich; trans. Ephraim Fischoff et al., Vol. 1, ch. 3. New York: Bedminster Press.

Weiss, Carol H. 1980. "Efforts at Bureaucratic Reform: What Have We Learned?" In *Making Bureaucracies Work*, eds. Carol H. Weiss and Allen H. Barton, 7–26. Beverly Hills: Sage.

White, Leonard D. 1926. *Introduction to the Study of Public Administration*. New York: Macmillan.

Wildavsky, Aaron. 1961. "Political Implications of Budgetary Reform." *Public Administration Review*, 21: 183–90.

Wilson, Woodrow. 1887. "The Study of Administration." *Political Science Quarterly*, 2: 197–222.

Chapter   4

ADMINISTRATIVE LIFE: PEOPLE IN ORGANIZATIONS

Organizations are social units created to attain one or more particular goals. In doing so, organizations limit individual behavior that may be dysfunctional to collaboration. The organization attempts to reduce uncertainty in human relationships and enhance predictability of individual behavior. By circumscribing individualistic actions, the organization attempts to minimize conflict and coordinate efforts of all members of the organization toward the common goal.

As attempts are made to bring together the values of the organization, individuals, and society, conflicts among them breed indeterminacy. The competing values create conflict and erosion of certainty, thus producing instability within. The cross-pressures from the environment lead to even greater swampy conditions. Faced with such uncertainty and pressure, individuals in the organization often return to what they know best. They become pathogenic in protecting their own interests as suggested in the previous chapter and become rigid and inflexible in attempting to find more stable footing.

At the same time organizations attempt to mold the behavior of individuals, the members of the organization seek fulfillment through it. Individuals join organizations for many reasons. Most join work organizations initially out of economic and physical necessity. Once their physical and economic needs are met, they may fulfill other needs through the organization. Through the work, they may achieve a sense of self-worth, accomplishment, or a feeling of being needed. The administrative process must accommodate both organizational and individual concerns.

Administrative organizations require individuals to work in groups. To accomplish the group's objectives means that the organization must establish goals, tasks, and procedures governing the interactions of members and must assign responsibilities and duties to each member of the organization.

The method by which procedures are established and activities assigned varies greatly by organization. In the case of public sector organizations, some external body such as a legislature or political executive establishes the basic purpose and rules for operation of the organization. However, each agency is usually given some discretion in how it will operate. Internal methods for determining procedures and assigning responsibilities differ greatly among organizations and will be discussed later in this chapter. What is important now is that the organization has the responsibility of establishing the framework for how the work is done. Most of our discussion deals with life in formal organizations, those which are created intentionally to accomplish some stated goal.

Individuals come to organizations with their own values and behavior patterns. As noted above, the organization attempts to control the behavior pattern in the interest of coordination of effort. As a result, an organization assumes an identity and consciousness of its own that differ from the summation of the behavior of its individual members. As Simon notes, individuals in a group are affected by a new force, the concern or consideration of the actions of others (Simon 1976). Freud studied the relationship of individual behavior to group interaction and found that groups have unexpected impact upon the behavior of individual adults (Freud 1955; Denhardt 1984).

THEORIES OF ORGANIZATION

While theories of organization have emphasized different elements of the organization, they continue to struggle with the same basic issues. The dominant issues are views of the roots of individual behavior, authority, and getting the individual to do what the organization needs done. Theoretical efforts continually redefine what is meant by organizational life, but they are cumulative in building upon one another. Management and organizations are characterized by complex relationships and behaviors. Relationships exist among individuals, organizations, subunits of organizations, superiors and subordinates, groups, and between organizations and their environments. This variety of relationships affects behavior of organizations and their members.

Stewart and Garson (1983) suggest five approaches to the study of organizations. A modification of their typology will be used here to illustrate the various ways individuals have been viewed relative to organizations. The five approaches to organizational behavior are: Classical, Human Relations, Decision Making, Organizational Humanism, and Human Systems. Each rests upon a different set of assumptions and expectations about human beings and their behavior.

Classical

The Classical approach to organization theory and behavior has its roots in the traditional public administration discussed in chapter 1. Weber's ideal construct of bureaucracy is consistent with the traditional roots and became a major theoretical justification for it. Basically, users of the approach assume a formal-legal framework for the organization. Authority is based upon law or formal rules, and work is structured according to a hierarchy of authority. Organization charts, rules and regulations, and job descriptions are relied upon for organizing the work. A major expression of the Classical approach is the Scientific Management School, which was intent upon increasing productivity and efficiency through systematic management. The leading proponent of Scientific Management was Frederick W. Taylor (1913), an engineer who turned his attention to the design of work. In terms of the individual, the Classical approach assumed that human beings are rational, are motivated by economic needs, and that payment for work is the best incentive.

Based on these assumptions about human nature, the Scientific Management School conducted empirical studies of the work situation to determine the one best way to perform any task. Proponents of the approach believed that they could discover universal laws for all activity; thus, management could determine what are the best processes for workers and train and direct the workers in performing those processes. Workers have little discretion in such a situation; instead they must learn standard operating procedures and apply them to work tasks.

To accomplish their objectives, the Scientific Management School conducted time and motion studies and job analyses. Worker tasks were studied in minute detail and those movements and actions that contributed to the organization's goals would be incorporated into the job while those that were counter productive would be eliminated. To encourage individuals to work at their highest levels of productivity, piece-rate incentives were incorporated into the pay scale.

Employees had an unanticipated reaction to these "scientific" approaches; they became dissatisfied. The very antagonism between labor and management which Taylor attempted to obviate through his scientific approach emerged in reaction to it. Eventually, under union pressure, the United States Congress prohibited the use of federal government monies in any time and motion studies that came to symbolize the Classical approach.

For the Classical theorists, organizations are defined by positions, which describe the tasks to be performed, instead of by the people in positions and by lines of authority and responsibility (hierarchy). Furthermore, the organization is formal and can be described by organizational charts and rules and regulations directing individual behavior. The way to make individual behavior compatible with organizational needs is to direct or order people to perform in specific ways. For the Classical theorists, human beings are valued for their physical abilities which fit the needs of the organization; the organization has no interest in the individual outside organizational activities. Management is supervisory and does not make policy, thus administration is separate from politics and authority is only formal and legal. Administrative efficiency is increased as specialization of the work process takes place (Gulick and Urwick 1937).

The Classical theorists looked at the organization as a rational instrument and assumed a congruence between personal and institutional rationality. The shortcoming of Classical theory is that it looks at only a small part of rationality (the means to a specific end) and a small part of individual behavior. It does not look at the whole range of actual behavior of people and attempt to fashion the organization around that reality. Instead, it attempts to mold individual behavior to the needs of the organization. Individuals are viewed as cogs in the organizational machine. Despite its shortcomings, Classical organization theory is evident in most large organizations in abundance. Position classification, for example, is still a key element of most large organizations as are formal rules and regulations, hierarchies of authority, and specialization of tasks.

Human Relations

Application of the principles of the Scientific Management School led to outright hostility by workers. As a result, industrial psychologists became part of the efficiency teams of management. The role of the industrial psychologist was to aid in the selection of the best employee, examine the effects of the work situation, and help to design optimum working conditions. The concerns of the industrial psychologist were the same as those of the Scientific Management School, namely, efficiency and productivity of the employee. As these new members of the team worked with management, however, they developed new ways of looking at efficiency and productivity. The findings of the industrial psychologists led to the development of the Human Relations School.

The beginnings of the Human Relations School are found in the Hawthorne Plant Studies of Western Electric in Chicago from 1927–1932 (Brown 1962; Homans 1951; Mayo 1933) although Mary Parker Follett had suggested similar ideas before this time (Follett 1924; Metcalf and Urwick 1940). The primary aim of the studies was to examine the work situation through scientific methods for purposes of developing greater productivity. Physical working conditions were considered to be the determinant of productivity of workers; thus, experiments were conducted with lighting and other physical aspects of the environment. The results were confusing in that changes in lighting in both directions (increased or decreased) seemed to have positive effects within limits. Similarly, other changes in the physical environment had conflicting results.

Consequently, the researchers decided that there must be something about the individuals' group interaction that is also of importance. They then began conducting interviews focusing on satisfaction of employees. They concluded that psychological and social factors are important to behavior and thus to productivity. In the interviewing it became apparent that individuals do not react as isolated beings but as social beings. This finding led industrial psychologists to analyze group dynamics. The informal organization by which people interacted with others within the formal organization became the object of much study (Blau 1963; Blau and Meyer 1971). The informal organization was viewed by the Human Relations approach as the most important element in promoting efficiency.

There are five principal conclusions that emerge from the Hawthorne Studies and form the basic foundation of the Human Relations School:

1. Social norms, not physical factors, are the most significant determinants of levels of production.

2. Behavior of workers is significantly affected by noneconomic sanctions and rewards.

3. Workers tend to react as members of groups rather than as individuals.

4. There is a need for leadership in creating and enforcing group norms different from the formal organizational leadership.

5. There is a need for democratic leadership and communication between levels of the organization and a need for participation by employees in decision making.

The Human Relations approach was accepted by many managers, but it was really an extension of the Scientific Management School. Human Relations resulted from the Scientific Management School's own studies and pursued the same goals, especially efficiency and productivity of the employee. Now the search for universal laws of productivity focused on laws of human behavior rather than on physical movements. Work was now seen as depending upon the psychological and social aspects of workers in organizations. During the 1950s, in particular, employers attempted to make the workplace a pleasant place to be and tried to create a family-type setting. Thus, office picnics and other activities to get employees and their families involved became common. To facilitate a sense of participation, suggestion boxes and other such efforts were developed. The problem with most such programs was that they gave the appearance of an interest in employees but often did not go beyond appearances. Once employees realized that the organization did not take suggestions seriously or did not want real participation, they became alienated.

The major change in work organizations fostered by the Human Relations approach was that it focused attention on the individual as a human being rather than as a cog in the organization. Organizations began to recognize that employees responded to other than monetary rewards and thus began the process of humanizing organizations. The implications for organizations were many. Authority was no longer only defined in terms of formal, rational factors. Instead informal, nonrational factors were also viewed as affecting authority relationships. While Scientific Management's goal of efficiency was still paramount, the issue now became how the individual worker could be induced to act the way the organization wanted through psychological and social means. Legitimate authority was now viewed in diverse ways.

In recognizing informal organizations within the formal structure, the Human Relations approach tended to ignore much of the formal authority relationship. A greater understanding of group dynamics resulted, and organization theory began to focus on social codes, group norms, perpetuation of informal groups and resistance to change as important elements in understanding behavior of individuals in organizations. In dealing with the individual, it also became apparent that security could be defined not only in terms of economics but also in terms of such things as status, prestige, and acceptance.

The Human Relations School searched for new ways of influencing human behavior to attain the greatest efficiency. They developed their own principles of group support, happiness of the worker, leadership, and supervision standards. The School strove for harmonious relationships without recognizing that such a situation is not always possible or preferable. The norms of human behavior became the all important standard, and any variance from that norm was viewed as dysfunctional. Thus, there developed a need for controlling variances through manipulation of the informal group. During the late 1940s and early 1950s, a challenge to the basic foundation of the Classical and Human Relations approaches arose in the form of more "scientific" Decision Making approaches.

Decision Making

While the Classical and Human Relations approaches focused on the same outcomes, they had strongly different orientations about how to achieve the most efficient operation of an organization. The Classical approach's focus on the need for rational behavior and the Human Relations' concern with the social and psychological needs of organization members placed the two approaches at polar extremes in terms of how to accomplish the goals of the organization. The tension between the rational needs of the organization and the nature of the individual gave rise to a new perspective as represented by the Decision Making approach. This approach recognized that there were conflicts between individual and organizational needs. While the perspective was new as applied to public administration, it had its foundation in the work of Mary Parker Follett (1924) who recognized the need for some mechanism other than traditional organization structure to coordinate human effort. She argued that cooperation and coordination of effort could not be directed or coerced, but that they come from the adjustments individuals make as they interact. Her work serves as a bridge between Classical perspectives and Decision Making approaches.

Herbert A. Simon is most closely identified with the Decision Making approach. In his *Administrative Behavior*, he develops a model of decision making that takes into account the inability of individuals to have complete information or even to use it if it were available. His model suggests organizing to enhance the flow of information and thus to improve decision making. Because individuals have incomplete information and limits to their ability to perform (Simon 1976), they "satisfice." Satisficing refers to doing what is acceptable given the ability of the individual and the information available. The organization member operates within the limits set by the organization and on the basis of individual skills, abilities, information, and understanding. The process of satisficing was further elaborated in Charles E. Lindblom's discussion of "muddling through" (Lindlom 1959). Muddling through is another name for the incremental approach in which decisions or actions occur as the result of limited comparison of alternatives that build upon past activity. As new needs or demands develop, administrators make adjustments to their decisions or policies. Rarely is there any full-scale change in direction or approach.

The Decision Making approach still relies upon a characterization of human beings as rational. While satisficing or muddling through, individuals were viewed as having a particular objective in mind and then making decisions relative to achievement of that objective. The underlying assumption remains that members of the organization will strive for accomplishment of its goals. The difference from earlier approaches, however, is that individuals were also viewed as having differing understandings of the goals and as being limited in their ability to act in concert with them. Limits to individual abilities lead to scaling down of goals and of looking to short-term accomplishments. Indeed, these short-term and scaled-down goals may be consistent with the organizational goals, but there may also be sidetracking and conflict.

For Simon, it was necessary for individuals to lose autonomy if they were to function well in the organization. Losing autonomy means that the individual accepts authoritatively made decisions of the manager and organization as legitimate. As with Barnard (1938), members of organizations are viewed as accepting the authority of superiors for differing reasons, among them what the individual perceives to be rational. Authority is thus based on the consent of subordinates to have power exercised over them by the superior within a particular range or zone. The organization sets the limits for individual action, and members are expected to accept rationality in terms of organizational needs. This point set the stage for a spirited debate with Chris Argyris and Herbert Simon over what they term "rational man organization theory" (Argyris 1973a, 1973b; Simon 1973). This debate reflects many of the concerns that emerged with the Organizational Humanists.

Organizational Humanism

Organizational Humanism has its roots in the Human Relations School, but it really goes much further. While the Human Relations School attempted to make the worker happy so as to serve the organization's needs, the Organizational Humanist approach concerns itself with the needs of the individual as well as the needs of the organization. Both should be addressed, according to the Organizational Humanists, but the health of the individual is given primacy.

The writings of Abraham Maslow (1954, 1962, 1965) provide the basic inspiration to the Organizational Humanists. His hierarchy of human needs (physiological, safety, love, esteem, and self-actualization) became the basis on which many organization theorists examined the relationship of the individual to the organization. Douglas McGregor (1960) is usually credited with adapting the hierarchy to an understanding of individuals in organizations. Basically, McGregor viewed the needs of the self-actualizing individual as being in conflict with the needs of the traditionally managed organization.

While McGregor examined the general relationship of the hierarchy of human needs to organizational needs, Chris Argyris went further and analyzed specific elements of the human personality relative to traditional organization (1964). His analysis focuses on the need of the mature human personality to move from passivity to activity, from dependence to independence, and from subordination to superordination. Further, he indicates that as individuals mature, they move from limited capacity to a wide range of capabilities, from shallow to in-depth understanding of things, from short-range to long-range perspectives, and from a lack of to a sense of self-awareness. Argyris argues that the demands of traditional management approaches are inconsistent with these tendencies of the mature human personality. Instead, traditional organizations require people to be dependent, passive, subordinate, and short range in perspective. Traditional management also provides very limited discretion to employees; therefore, they use limited capabilities, have little understanding of the larger implications of what they do and subordinate their own identity to the needs of the organization. The conflict between mature personality needs and organizational needs results in various modes of accommodation including intellectual separation of work and nonwork life, alienation from the organization, and possibly sabotage. The traditional approach also discourages individuals from taking responsibility for their work and fosters using rules, regulations, or policy as excuses for continuing old practices or for not doing something.

The conflicts between individual and organizational needs led to a great deal of study of matches between particular personality types and organizations. Typologies of individuals and how they adjusted to organizational environments and demands became popular. Robert Presthus (1978) characterized individuals as upward mobiles, indifferents, and ambivalents while Anthony Downs (1967) viewed them as climbers, conservers, zealots, advocates, and statesmen. Other typologies include what Maccoby terms "the craftsman, jungle fighter, company man, and gamesman" (Maccoby 1976) and what Gouldner refers to as the "cosmopolitans and locals" (Gouldner 1957).

These typologies are based upon how individuals seek power and success in the organization, their views and understanding of organizational activities, self-interest, cause orientation, approach to authority, or other mode of behavior that differentiates one person from another. Some people are so intent upon succeeding in the organization that they completely buy into the organization's values (upward mobiles, climbers, company man). Others accept the demands of the organization as necessary to earn economic security or the like although they may not agree with all that they are asked to do in the organization (indifferents). Still others have strong values that are often in conflict with the organization's norms, but they attempt to work within the organization, often with great frustration (ambivalents, zealots). While these typologies are interesting and helpful for characterizing behavior, there has been very little rigorous analysis to substantiate their existence. Thus, it is best to use them as guides to understand kinds of behavior rather than molds into which every member of an organization can be fit neatly.

These typologies have called attention to the fact that people respond differently to organizations and their demands upon the individual. As a result, organization theory has moved to a formal consideration of the individual as a variable within the organization. The Organizational Humanists have been concerned with humanizing the organization because of their concern with the integrity of the individual as much as for the interests of the organization. The tone of the Organizational Humanists actually suggests that the well-being of the individual is most important and organizations reap benefits through greater productivity of healthy individuals.

More importantly, Organizational Humanists accept the idea that there are consistencies between the objectives of the organization and the needs of the individual. The key is to recognize that there are ways of organizing work to capitalize on the compatibility of organizational and individual needs. Because the Organizational Humanists view work as a natural part of the human condition, people are viewed as interested in it. They are motivated by factors intrinsic to the work itself. They are achievement oriented and thus respond positively to opportunities to experience a sense of accomplishment. Further, positive work incentives are available: delegating responsibility, allowing of discretion, independence of judgment on the job, and the opportunity to participate and be creative (McGregor 1960; Blake and Mouton 1964; Bennis 1973).

Organizational humanists stressed democratic values within the organization, including full and free communication among individuals regardless of rank or power. Consensus rather than coercion should govern decision making because it fosters compromise as a means of managing conflict. Influence is based upon competence and expertise rather than the possession of formal power. While Organizational Humanists recognize that human

needs and organizational needs may be in conflict, they emphasized the rational resolution of these conflicts while maintaining
the dignity of the individual person (Bennis and Slater 1968). Concerns of the Organizational Humanists are primarily internal to the
organization. In later years, the New Public Administration expanded the concern with democracy to include external factors. In
the New Public Administration, organizations are viewed as instruments for increasing societal as well as internal democracy.

The humanizing of the organization is rooted in the delineation
of differences between traditional and more contemporary views of
human nature as suggested by McGregor's Theory X and Theory Y
construct (1960). Theory X outlines the basic assumptions about
human nature according to Classical management approaches. In
this system, people are assumed to be inherently lazy and to shun
work when possible. Further, people fear punishment and depriva-
tion. These fears impel people to work and are used by management as a means of directing, controlling, and motivating workers.
Theory X also assumes that people prefer to be dependent and
want security most of all; thus, incentives are those things that
contribute to security.

McGregor's Theory Y assumes that the expenditure of physical
effort is a natural part of human nature and that punishment and
external control are not the only or necessarily the best motivators.
People will work toward a goal to which they are committed.
Achievement brings rewards of its own and engenders further commitment. Additionally, the average person learns to accept and to
seek responsibility and, given the opportunity to be creative and to
use initiative, will demonstrate a wide range of abilities. For Theory
Y, which is the basis of the Organizational Humanists' approach,
the organization ought to take advantage of these characteristics of
people. More democratic and humane organizations are the result.

Human Systems

Contemporary organization theory, dating from the mid-1960s,
is manifested in a variety of concerns arising from the other traditions. In effect, contemporary theory synthesizes elements from
many of the earlier approaches. To a great extent, contemporary
approaches use Systems theory as a focal point for understanding
organizations and their activities. Systems theory views organiza-

tions as being composed of interrelated parts which affect one another and adapt to environmental changes. Katz and Kahn (1966) articulately examine the organization as a social system that interacts with its environment and is affected internally by elements from the environment. This open systems approach provides the basis for much of current analysis of organizations although a systems theory basis is not always explicitly acknowledged.

Contemporary theory treats organizations as complex units in which a variety of relationships exist. Those relationships are affected by formal, structural aspects of the organization as well as by informal, behavioral factors. Furthermore, the organization cannot be understood without reference to the larger system in which it operates (the environment).

James Thompson (1967) carries the Human Systems theory further by using it in both closed and open forms for understanding organizations. Closed systems have clearly identifiable boundaries and highly structured and predictable activities. Open systems are much more complex, with constantly changing interactions within the organization and with the environment. Thus, open systems are much less predictable. By focusing on the closed system, it is possible to analyze organizations in their rational approach to goals from an internal perpsective. Thus, for some purposes, it is possible and important to understand that organizations act without reference to their environments. At other times, it is necessary to understand environmental influences on organizations in order to have a complete picture of the organization. Some of its activities are accommodations to environmental influences. Particularly when it comes to survival, public sector organizations develop strategies to accommodate the environment. Even within the organization, the open system approach is important in understanding informal organizations (those networks and interactions developed by organization members on their own) and their relationship to the formal organization. According to Thompson, management would like to operate as a closed system, but reality makes it impossible to do so.

Concerns of contemporary theorists differ from earlier theorists in that the individual is viewed in a dual role as part of the organization and as part of society as a whole. There are conflicts between organizational and social roles which become centered in the individual. As a result, contemporary theory often examines the struggles individuals have in making those roles compatible. Alienation of the worker from the organization is often emphasized along with efforts to eliminate alienation and conflict. Organization Development theorists (Argyris and Schon 1978; Golembiewski and Eddy 1978) view conflict as natural and search for ways to manage it to the advantage of the organization. By reducing the barriers to communication, organizations can create better understanding among their members and through participation in the management process, members become committed to organizational objectives. Organization Development techniques are viewed as ways of integrating the needs of the individual and the organization.

Additionally, there is mutual dependence between the individual and organization. Contemporary theorists recognize this interdependence—each needs the other for certain purposes. The organization functions as a result of the mutual accommodation of individual and organizational needs.

Beyond the concerns with individual and organizational behavior, modern theorists deal with many other concerns. During the 1970s, there was much discussion of the New Public Administration (Marini 1971; Frederickson 1974; Harmon 1981). One of the basic premises of the New Public Administration is that public agencies ought to foster social justice. The approach also focuses on democratizing the internal workings of the organization. The New Public Administration advocates suggest that new values such as equal employment opportunity, social equity, and clientelism replace organizational rationality as goals. Their argument is that traditional public administration favors those who have access to power and politics; thus, those who most need government protection and service are left out of the system. This perspective raises questions about whom organizations are designed to serve. While the New Public Administration has sensitized academics and public administrators to social equity issues, it has not revolutionized the public administration community in the way its advocates might have expected.

There are many critiques of the New Public Administration that raise questions about its efficacy. Mosher (1968) suggests that the goal of internal democracy in public organizations is a noble one, but that it could lead to a more fundamental problem for democracy. Carried to its fullest extent, internal democracy could lead to the bureaucrats deciding what the purpose of the organization is. This situation would be in conflict with the idea of democratic control by those elected by the citizens to establish purposes for governmental organizations.

Michael Harmon and Richard Mayer (1986), advocates of the New Public Administration values, concede that the issues raised by Mosher have not been totally resolved. They suggest that it is not realistic to expect a complete resolution because democracy implies competing values. Their argument is that the New Public Administration has forced the field of public administration to address the normative questions raised by the movement and has caused a continuing examination of the purposes of public organizations. It has also provided a framework in which the tensions between the traditional theorists and the Organizational Humanists can be clarified.

When looking at organizations, it is clear that all these approaches to organization theory and behavior are in use. All organizations adapt elements of the various approaches. Even the most democratic and humane organization seldom has the liberty to be concerned only with the needs of its members. It has a goal or goals to accomplish yet the needs of the individual have to be accommodated. The issue often becomes how humane and democratic the organization can be while still accomplishing its purpose.

The empirical evidence on the effectiveness of different organization approaches is difficult to evaluate. Not surprisingly, successful experiments of companies or government agencies using a particular approach often receive a great deal of media and case-study attention. Failures of innovative approaches seldom get widely reported. There have been some in-depth studies, however, which shed light on the applicability of the more contemporary approaches. Dubin (1959), for example, concludes that not all people are suited for or interested in organizations based upon Organizational Humanism. Instead, many prefer to have clear directives from management. Every worker has different needs and values; consequently, no one form of or approach to organizing work is appropriate for everyone. In his own study of an industrial organization, Dubin found that only 10 percent of industrial workers preferred independence.

Similarly, Kaplan and Tausky (1977) reviewed the research on Organizational Humanism and concluded that many of its precepts had to be accepted cautiously if at all. Their evaluation of studies suggested that while professional employees were likely to benefit from application of humanistic management approaches, manual labor and lower-salaried workers were not. Manual labor and lower-salaried workers tend to derive satisfaction off the job and not at work. People have widely different reasons for working and seek different things from work; the evidence does not support the idea that people view work as inherently interesting. Many of the other tenets of Organizational Humanism are challenged by Kaplan and Tausky. Despite the questions about the tenets and empirical validation of the humanistic approach, it is having an impact on the way public sector agencies conduct their business (Rosenbloom 1986).

MOTIVATION AND MANAGEMENT STYLES

Motivation

As the previous discussion indicates, different things motivate different people. Organizations attempt to encourage particular types of behavior. In order to do so, it is necessary to address the great variation in human motivation. Our discussion of major organization theories focused upon assumptions about human nature. From those assumptions, theorists and those applying the theories also made assumptions about what would motivate people to do what the organization desired. For the Classical theorists, people could be motivated by addressing economic needs; thus, the primary motivator was believed to be money. Increased pay for increased productivity was the mechanism used.

For the Human Relations School, social and psychological factors were used to motivate people. Social needs were viewed as the key to productivity and were satisfied by social interaction. Therefore, Human Relations managers relied upon creating a sense of social support by appearing to care for the employee and by encouraging group activity.

Modern motivation theory, symbolized by Organizational Humanism and Human Systems, usually pays homage to Maslow's hierarchy of needs. Each need is a motivator as long as it is unfulfilled. Once fulfilled, it no longer motivates and the next higher need becomes a motivator. While Maslow's hierarchy has provided the foundation of much of the contemporary literature on human motivation, it has also led to some confusion. Many theorists suggest that each need has to be satisfied in order while others stress that the level of needs of any one individual varies over time. Among those building upon Maslow's hierarchy is Frederick Herzberg (1966) who believed that motivation comes from within and that organizations need to use positive growth factors to encourage employees to produce. He claims that organizations tend to focus on "hygiene" factors such as physical surroundings, status, salary, and administrative rules and regulations, which all members of the organization expect anyway and thus are not effective motivators. Instead, opportunity for advancement, achievement, and increasing responsibility, the nature of the job, and recognition are factors that motivate workers. In order to motivate employees, organizations are encouraged to design work so as to emphasize the motivators.

Employees come to organizations socialized to particular attitudes and values that also affect motivation (Eddy 1981). Some people develop strong work ethics and are satisfied with nothing less than their best effort; others may feel the need to do no more than is necessary to get by. Many employees need to be stroked and have a need for approval while others have a need for independence and the opportunity to achieve on their own terms. Some have a need for exercising responsibility and discretion and a sense of accomplishment. Others may want money or symbols of success such as titles and accoutrements of office. Clearly, one approach to motivating employees is not going to be successful with these and many other needs that characterize members of every organization. The key for management is in linking individual needs and action to the achievement of organizational goals. Understanding what motivates individual employees is the major first step.

Management

Management refers to the ability of supervisors and managers to obtain the cooperation of the members of their organization in the accomplishment of organizational goals. There are many factors which affect management including leadership, formal authority, persuasion, interpersonal activities, the situation, and communication. Furthermore managers have a number of tools such as decision making, information processing, budgeting, planning, and personnel systems to assist them in management. How effectively managers use these tools may well determine their success.

Much of management depends upon the ability of managers to get employees to suspend their own judgment and accept the manager's leadership (Barnard 1938). Employees act on the basis of habit, their own self-interest and values, and what they believe to be rational. In order to get employees to change or to comply with management directives, it is necessary to make management desires as consistent as possible with those of the individual employee. A key to such effort is often assumed to be leadership abilities of the manager.

Moral codes are also important to the acceptance of a manager's directives (Barnard 1938). All individuals have a moral code which delimits their behavior. When management or the organization demand activities in conflict with the subordinate's moral code, he or she is not likely to accept authority. The strength of commitment to the moral code will affect whether the subordinate will accept the authority as legitimate. Furthermore, the subordinate's views of the manager's moral code are also important in that we expect managers to provide moral leadership.

Managerial styles vary greatly and are generally assumed to influence the success of organizational activity (Eddy 1981). Styles range from autocratic/authoritarian to democratic/participative. White and Lippitt (1968) have conducted some of the most exhaustive studies of leadership and management styles. They experimented with adult leaders of boys clubs using three different leadership styles—authoritarian, democratic, and laissez-faire. In their experiments, the authoritarian style appeared to be most effective in the short run and as long as the leader was present. The democratic style appeared to be more effective in the long run as people continued to perform even in the absence of the leader. The laissez-faire approach, in which the leader provides no real guidance, seemed to be ineffective.

Others have developed variations on the themes suggested by White and Lippitt. Blake and Mouton (1964), for example, use a two-dimensional grid to examine management styles. The two axes of the grid are task emphasis and people emphasis. The task emphasis refers to focusing on the technical, operational aspects of task accomplishment while the people emphasis focuses on human relations and motivation based on Organizational Humanism. Their conclusion, and that of much related research, is that the most effective approach is a combination of the two emphases. Managers who score highly on both dimensions tend to make the best managers and combine the task orientation with good people skills. Sandra Blem (1977) has developed a two-dimensional typology based on similar orientations. Calling hers the androgyny concept, Blem views managers as tough and assertive or as nurturing and relationship oriented. As with the Blake and Mouton grid, evidence suggests that a combination of the two styles is most effective (Sargent 1978).

The lesson for managers to learn from research on styles is that they must be very adaptable. They need to adapt to different types of employees with differing needs. The research also indicates that managers need to combine a rational goal orientation with concern for their employees. Thus, it is necessary to be task oriented but also to understand employees and actively listen and allow participation in what is being done. These combinations of efforts seem to lead to the greatest success. There is, however, no magic formula for good management and different styles may have varying effects depending upon the situation in which they are used.

ADMINISTRATIVE COMMUNICATION

As Simon (1976) notes, communication is the instrument for linking behaviors of individuals in groups and thus is important in eliciting cooperative effort. There is no question that effective communication is critical to the ability of managers to manage. Nonetheless, communication is often taken for granted and, therefore, is often very ineffective.

Communication may be characterized in a variety of ways. It may be examined in terms of whether it is formal or informal, interpersonal or organizational, by direction of flow, whether internal or external, and in terms of problems associated with it.

Formal and Informal

Formal communication refers to communication that is based in some particular organizational purpose. Some authoritative member of the organization attempts to communicate with a particular audience, through appropriate channels, to accomplish the goals of the organization (Gordon 1986). Informal communication, on the other hand, is likely to be interpersonal and less structured. It is also likely to derive from many different sources and its intended audience and purpose are not necessarily consistent with organizational goals. While many managers concentrate on formal communication and pay little attention to the informal, they probably do so at their own peril. Informal communication is important to holding the organization together because it represents networks among people who have to work together. It often helps facilitate the work of the organization by speeding up the communication process and building a sense of community among workers.

Informal communication can also be destructive to the organization to the extent that it undermines managerial authority. Effective managers normally accept the inevitability of informal communication and utilize its channels when possible for furthering organizational goals. The Human Relations School placed a great deal of emphasis on informal communication and networking.

Communication Flow

Traditional management approaches usually assumed that the only really important communication in an organization is that which flows downward through the hierarchy. Downward communication is important for managers to let the rest of the organization know policy and what to do. Thus, downward communication is often in the form of information sharing and directives on how to comply with new policy and rules and regulations. Obviously, it is important in keeping members throughout the organization informed.

Upward communication is just as important as downward. Through upward communication, it is possible for managers high in the hierarchy to find out what is going on below. It is an important channel for learning about problems with policy or other aspects of the organization. Some upward channels are created for collecting particular kinds of information; others encourage employees to voice their concerns and suggestions. Effective managers normally encourage open channels of communication from every level of the organization.

Lateral (horizontal) communication is also very important because it cuts across authority lines and fosters voluntary coordina-

tion. Lateral communication permits people in one part of the organization to know speedily and at low cost what those in another
part need or are doing. Usually, parts of organizations are interdependent and rely upon other units to accomplish certain tasks to
facilitate their own. Communication across unit lines permits units
to learn what they can do to facilitate the other's work. Of course,
such a purpose is the ideal; often the result is just the opposite in
that units may work at cross-purposes or refuse to cooperate.

Lateral communication is also significant in building a sense of
community in the organization. By learning about other elements
of the organization and how specialized tasks fit into the complete
picture, employees may identify more closely with the organization. They may also develop an attachment to the members of the
organization as a group pursuing the same purposes.

All organizations share in having communication flows in all
three directions. Some are encouraged more than others. In some
organizations, managers attempt to open lines of communication
as much as possible while in others there are tendencies to maintain very formal channels with limited access. Contemporary organization theorists normally suggest expanding channels as much as
possible as a way of involving members in the organization.

Internal and External

Normally when organizational communication is discussed, we
think in terms of internal communication. In most organizations,
the vast majority of communication is internal with management
using it to hold the organization together and on track in pursuit of
its goals. External communication is also an important element in
that it is used to keep those outside the organization informed of
what is happening. This form of communication is particularly
important in the public sector where citizens and clientele depend
upon the services of the public agency.

External communication may be interpreted as public relations
and often is handled officially by a public information office in the
public sector. The purpose of external communication is to keep
the public informed of services and programs. Often, however, the
process is used to generate understanding and good will toward
the organization. When the purpose is more to ensure the survival
of the agency or program than to provide a needed service, exter-

nal communication is abused. Another abuse may be the use of external communication to generate public support for larger budgets and the like. There are many ways in which such efforts take place. The friendly military base does not provide open house, fly municipal and state officials to meetings, and encourage civic involvement of its officers only out of a commitment to service. Rather, there are likely to be payoffs in the form of important support for its facilities and programs as a result of these activities. Other public agencies have different things to offer members of the public and utilize them for the same types of purposes.

External communication has also become problematic in many government agencies because of attempts to withhold particular information. It is only natural that an agency would not want to release information that is detrimental to its cause. Since the agency also is likely to be the only one knowing what information is available, there is a lot of control implied by this power over information. In recent years, freedom of information acts at the national and state levels, along with open-meetings legislation, have opened information up to a great extent, but there are still many problems.

In reality, top-level management is often unaware of many aspects of external communication. People within the organization, especially at middle-management levels, communicate constantly with counterparts in other similar organizations. Often the communication occurs between and among organizations within the same governmental jurisdiction. At other times, similar units in different cities or different states exchange information. Managers in the Department of Corrections, for example, deal with managers in counterpart organizations in other states on a regular basis. Associations of professionals in similar jobs also provide much opportunity for lateral communication of information. Such communication is often very effective in facilitating the work of the organization in that managers can take advantage of the experiences of others with particular situations or problems. At the same time, however, this form of communication has the potential for undermining the authority of top-level management. Middle-level managers have the opportunity to present strong cases for their perspectives from the experience of fellow professionals and there is no assurance that the information is representative of all similar organizations.

Communications Problems

Among the most important problems with communication are lack of clarity and access to information. For managers, it is important to state things clearly so that everyone understands the communication in the way it was intended. Virtually everyone has played the game where a statement is passed around the room by whispering in the ear of the person sitting in the next chair. By the time the statement gets around the room, it is very likely to be changed and often communicates something completely different from the original statement. The same happens in organizations. If a message is not stated in simple, straightforward language, it is likely to mean many different things as it is passed from one level or unit to another. This is the problem of interpretation. People respond differently to the same words, and as they translate messages, they give those messages new meaning.

Access to information is another major problem. When channels of communication are limited and information is kept under wraps, members of the organization have a difficult time knowing what is going on. More importantly, very limited channels of communication have the potential for screening out information. The manager at the top of the organization may receive incomplete information if it goes up only through specified channels. At each level, it is possible that some information will be screened out, especially if it puts the one screening it in a bad light. At times, some managers may just assume, as well, that certain information is not important to pass along. This screening of information can place upper-level managers in awkward positions of not having complete information for making decisions. Similar screening can occur in downward and lateral communication. On the other hand, if too much information is communicated, channels become overloaded and people ignore some of the information.

Organizations in the mid-1980s enjoy technology not dreamed of just a few years ago. With electronic and computer technology, organizations are able to collect, store, analyze, and disseminate information at amazing speed. Along with these advantages come problems as well. Privacy of information is problematic given the large amount of material stored on any individual in a variety of places. Access to the information is not always secure, and people who have ulterior motives can often obtain it.

Government agencies usually adopt the new technology with the belief that it will reduce cost and staff, improve supervision, and provide better information for problem solving. While it does have the potential to help, some analysts believe the new technology has been oversold (Danziger 1977) and that it is often bought uncritically. Overzealous purchase of such equipment without evaluation of needs can be wasteful. Kraemer and Dutton (1979) also found that use of new technology often becomes a resource for those in power to use to stay in power. They can use it to resist the efforts of those who want to change. By having a monopoly on use of the equipment, they can claim that a proposed change in procedure or policy would incur prohibitive costs, thus killing enthusiasm for the change.

DEMOCRATIC ADMINISTRATION

The New Public Administration and Organizational Humanists proposed an administrative system that would incorporate democratic values and practices into the operation of organizations. In suggesting change, the New Public Administration advocated participative management, democratization of the decision-making process, and humanization of the work situation. They also proposed that clients have the opportunity to help define and implement programs. Many organization theorists were very optimistic that bureaucracy would become increasingly democratized because of its increasing professionalization, education, and socialization (Berkley 1971; Bennis and Slater 1968). While their expectations have not been met, there are many attempts to democratize organizational life in the public sector. The traditional, hierarchical structure still dominates, but some change has taken place.

Most advocates of democratic administration start with a discussion of participative management. Participation by employees in the management process follows the Organizational Humanists' suggestions that individuals have the capability and desire to assume responsibility. Michael Smith (1976) notes that there are many reasons organizations should adopt participative approaches. Among these reasons is that participative management facilitates interpersonal social and political skills of employees which results in better interaction with the public. Members of an organization are also more likely to assume responsibility for their actions if they participate in the decisions leading to them. They are less likely to attempt to avoid the responsibility and accountability for them. Smith also believes that participative management decreases the amount of time and energy wasted on resentment of the boss. Because decision making and responsibility are diffused, contacts with the public are also diffused, and there is the potential for greater responsiveness. Additionally, participation by members of the organization may result in better decisions. For example, in selecting people for promotion, member participation is likely to result in choices based on competence, ability, and merit. Of course, a negative effect may be that only those who conform to organizational norms get chosen, resulting in stagnation.

Although these are all persuasive arguments for adoption of democratic administration, they have not resulted in a dramatic change in organizations. Smith (1976) attributes the lack of success to the resistance of management to give up power, independence, and the strength of their standard operating procedures. Top-level administrators are also viewed as perceiving themselves to be elites (public guardians) as opposed to the rank and file. There is a tendency among administrators to attempt to protect the organization from the uncertainty of the outside world and that tendency reinforces traditional ways of doing things. Smith recognizes that some accommodations are made through introduction of some democratic practices but does not find evidence of full participative management in public sector organizations.

Stewart and Garson (1983) suggest three other, although overlapping, impediments to participative management. They indicate that public organizations' accountability to the political environment breeds protectionism and thus reliance on traditional approaches. Additionally, the fact that goals of public sector organizations are often unclear and difficult to measure makes it difficult to demonstrate that participative management or any alternative is effective. Finally, they suggest that public agencies resist participative management because of the general belief that elected political leaders are supposed to make policy decisions. Employees of bureaucracy are supposed to be implementing policy and not deciding what the policy should be.

Participative management approaches have been more common in the private sector than in public agencies. Nonetheless, there are a few approaches which have been utilized in government bureaucracy. Among the prominent approaches is management by objectives (MBO) which has been used by agencies at all levels of government. Basically, MBO involves participation by members of the organization in the establishment of goals with plans for accomplishing them (Drucker 1954). In complete MBO programs, employees also participate in deciding how best to use resources and in seeing that activities are kept on track. MBO also implies evaluation of results for consistency with organizational purposes and effectiveness. Ultimately, the evaluation process is used to provide feedback to the decision-making process. As Newland (1976) indicates, however, most MBO experiments in the national government have been streamlined versions of the process involving only the setting of objectives, monitoring progress, and evaluating results. Zero base budgeting (ZBB) is a variation on the same theme which gained a great deal of popularity during the late 1970s. It permitted participation at the lower levels of the organization in the creation of decision packages that were the building blocks of the budget and thus policy for the governmental unit.

Another recent addition to participative management is the Quality Circle (QC). Quality Circles actually originated in the United States in the 1940s but were not viewed favorably by industry or government until utilized successfully in Japan. Adopted by the Japanese after World War II as a quality control tool, QCs became popular there in the 1960s and 1970s and were reimported to the United States in the 1970s. The Quality Circle consists of a work group that attempts to work out organizational problems. In the work setting, they have now come to include all types of organizational problems, not just quality control. Quality Circles average eight people who meet regularly to discuss work issues with the intent of finding ways to resolve problems. Supervisors or lead workers are included in the circles. Although there is much lore about their success in Japan, some studies have suggested that other organizations in Japan not using QCs have been just as successful (Cole 1979). The important point about QCs is that they represent a form of participative management, and they have been reported to work in many instances. As with any other innovation, QCs may not work in all situations.

Organization Development (OD) is a humanistic approach that has been utilized to solve problems in work organizations. Building upon the model of the Organizational Humanists, OD attempts to break down organizational barriers to effective work (Golembiew-ski and Eddy 1978). In particular, OD focuses on opening up the communication process and encouraging participation by all members of the organization in its decisions. The approach is based upon the assumption that if all members participate in an open problem-solving atmosphere, they would be better employees. By open communication, people are supposed to develop greater self-awareness and awareness of others, resulting in greater trust and commitment to the group's activities. Many public sector organizations do use OD, but there are practical limits to its use because of external politics and fiscal constraints which hurt any innovation. There are also many disagreements about the utility and ethics of such programs thus causing many managers to be cautious.

Theory Z is yet another approach to organizing based upon Organizational Humanism (Ouchi and Jaeger 1978). Essentially, it is the same as Theory Y in its basic assumptions and attempts to improve organizational performance through the same mechanisms as Organization Development. The basic difference from OD is that Theory Z adds the concept of permanent rather than short-term employment and career path considerations. As far as the internal processes are concerned, however, Theory Z follows the same type of guidelines as OD.

Another form of participative management that is used very extensively in public as well as private sector organizations is bargaining. Collective bargaining, or labor management relations as it is often called, allows for democratic participation to the extent that it provides for representation of the interests of the worker. These interests are legitimized by a formal process in which representatives of employees negotiate and reach agreement with management over issues of importance to both. Additionally, procedures are developed for insuring against arbitrary action against individual employees and for resolution of grievances brought against either party to the bargaining. Grievances are usually handled by outside neutral parties, thus increasing the protections against arbitrariness. While many managers complain that the bargaining model undermines their authority, it may also aid them in communicating with employees because the union leadership becomes the mechanism for communication. Although considered a form of democratization of the work place, bargaining can also become very ritualized and individual participation can get lost in the shuffle. Oftentimes, individual members feel that the union is taken over by the leadership and loses touch with the interests of the rank and file.

Codetermination has developed as another mechanism for employees to have a formal voice in work organizations in Europe, particularly Yugoslavia and West Germany. Basically, it involves equal representation of workers and management on boards of directors. Work councils of employees are also often created. The boards and work councils have a greater deal of power over working conditions. While codetermination is popular in Germany, it is not used in the United States at the present time although it is becoming increasingly common to have labor representatives on boards of directors of private firms.

Administrative democracy is a popular concept in the literature, but research indicates that it is rather limited in application. Most public bureaucracies continue to be dominated by hierarchical organizations with limited employee participation in the decision making. Nonetheless, organizations have become increasingly sensitive to employee needs and behavioral concerns over the past two or three decades. There are much greater opportunities for participation, and many employees find it possible to exercise discretion, independence, and creativity as parts of their jobs.

During the 1960s, democratic administration was extended to include the general public in the decision-making process. Many of the War on Poverty and other social programs required participation by recipients of services or members of neighborhoods affected by the programs. Committees and councils of interested persons became partners in the implementation of policies. While the experiments worked well in many places, they also generated a lot of abuse and opposition from local elected officials who felt that they were being bypassed in the process.

Public administrators conduct their activities through organizations, and the public and elected representatives expect results from those organizations. In order to produce results, public agencies need resources and processes to assist them in addition to working with people. The next chapter turns to an examination of those resources and processes.

REFERENCES

Argyris, Chris. 1964. *Integrating the Individual and Organization*. New York: Wiley.

Argyris, Chris. 1973a. "Some Limits of Rational Man Organizational Theory." *Public Administration Review*, 33: 253–267.

Argyris, Chris. 1973b. "Organization Man: Rational *and* Self-Actualizing." *Public Administration Review*, 33: 354–357.

Argyris, Chris, and Donald Schon. 1978. *Organizational Learning: A Theory of Action Perspective*. Reading, Mass.: Addison-Wesley.

Barnard, Chester I. 1938. *The Functions of the Executive*. Cambridge: Harvard University Press.

Bennis, Warren. 1973. *Beyond Bureaucracy*. New York: McGraw-Hill.

Bennis, Warren G., and Philip E. Slater. 1968. *The Temporary Society*. New York: Harper & Row.

Berkley, George E. 1971. *The Administrative Revolution*. Englewood Cliffs, N.J.: Prentice-Hall.

Blake, Robert R., and Jane S. Mouton. 1964. *The Managerial Grid*. Houston: Gulf Publishing.

Blau, Peter. 1963. *The Dynamics of Bureaucracy: A Study of Interpersonal Relationships in Two Government Agencies*, 2nd ed. Chicago: University of Chicago Press.

Blau, Peter, and Marshall W. Mayer. 1971. *Bureaucracy in Modern Society*. 2d. ed. New York: Random House.

Blem, Sandra Lipsitz. 1977. "Psychological Androgyny." In *Beyond Sex Roles*, ed. Alice G. Sargent, 319–324. St. Paul: West Publishing.

Brown, J. A. C. 1962. *The Social Psychology of Industry*. Baltimore: Penguin.

Cole, Robert. 1979. *Work, Mobility and Participation*. Berkeley: University of California Press.

Danziger, James N. 1977. "Computers, Local Governments, and the Litany to EDP." *Public Administration Review*, 37: 28–37.

Denhardt, Robert B. 1984. *Theories of Public Organization*. Monterey, Calif.: Brooks/Cole.

Downs, Anthony. 1967. *Inside Bureaucracy*. Boston: Little, Brown.

Drucker, Peter F. 1954. *The Practice of Management*. New York: Harper & Row.

Dubin, Robert. 1959. "Person and Organizations." *Proceedings of the 11th Annual Meeting of the Industrial Relations Research Association*. 1959: 160–163.

Eddy, William B. 1981. *Public Organization Behavior and Development*. Cambridge, Mass.: Winthrop.

Follett, Mary Parker. 1924. *Creative Experience*. New York: Longmans, Green.

Frederickson, H. George, ed. 1974. "A Symposium: Social Equity and Public Administration." *Public Administration Review*, 34: 1–51.

Freud, Sigmund. 1955. *The Origin and Development of Psychoanalysis*. Chicago: Regnerry.

Golembiewski, Robert T., and William Eddy, eds. 1978. *Organization Development in Public Administration, Part I*. New York: Marcel Dekker.

Gordon, George J. 1986. *Public Administration in America*. 3d ed. New York: St. Martin's Press.

Gouldner, Alvin W. 1957. "Cosmopolitans and Locals: Toward an Analysis of Latent Social Roles." *Administrative Science Quarterly*, 2: 281–292.

Gulick, Luther, and Lyndall Urwick, eds. 1937. *Papers on the Science of Administration*. New York: Institute of Public Administration.

Harmon, Michael M. 1981. *Action Theory for Public Administration*. New York: Longman.

Harmon, Michael M., and Richard T. Mayer. 1986. *Organization Theory for Public Administration*. Boston: Little, Brown.

Herzberg, Frederick. 1966. *Work and the Nature of Man*. Cleveland: World Publishing.

Homans, George C. 1951. "The Western Electric Research." In *Human Factors in Management*, rev. ed., ed. Schuyler Dean Hoslett. New York: Harper & Row.

Kaplan, H. Roy, and Curt Tausky. 1977. "Humanism in Organizations: A Critical Appraisal." *Public Administration Review*, 37: 171–180.

Katz, Daniel, and Robert L. Kahn. 1966. *The Social Psychology of Organizations*. New York: Wiley.

Kraemer, Kenneth L., and William H. Dutton. 1979. "The Interests Served by Technological Reform: The Case of Computing." *Administration and Society*, 11: 80–106.

Lindblom, Charles E. 1959. "The Science of Muddling Through." *Public Administration Review*, 19: 79–88.

Maccoby, Michael. 1976. *The Gamesman: The New Corporate Leaders*. New York: Simon & Schuster.

McGregor, Douglas. 1960. *The Human Side of Enterprise*. New York: McGraw-Hill.

Marini, Frank, ed. 1971. *Toward a New Public Administration: The Minnowbrook Perspective*. Scranton, Pa.: Chandler.

Maslow, Abraham. 1954. *Motivation and Personality*. New York: Harper and Brothers.

Maslow, Abraham. 1962. *Toward a Psychology of Being*. Princeton, N.J.: Van Nostrand.

Maslow, Abraham. 1965. *Eupsychian Management*. Homewood, Ill.: Richard D. Irwin.

Mayo, Elton. 1933. *The Human Problems of an Industrial Civilization*. New York: Macmillan.

Metcalf, Henry C., and Lyndall Urwick, eds. 1940. *Dynamic Administration: The Collected Works of Mary Parker Follett*. New York: Harper & Row.

Mosher, Frederick C. 1968. *Democracy and the Public Service*. New York: Oxford University Press.

Newland, Chester A. 1976. "Policy/Program Objectives and Federal Management: The Search for Government Effectiveness." *Public Administration Review*, 36: 20–27.

Ostrom, Vincent. 1974. *The Intellectual Crisis in American Public Administration*. rev. ed. University, Ala.: University of Alabama Press.

Ouchi, William G., and Alfred M. Jaeger. 1978. "Type Z Organization—Stability in the Midst of Mobility." *Academy of Management Review* 3: 305–314.

Presthus, Robert. 1978. *The Organizational Society*. rev. ed. New York: St. Martin's Press.

Rosenbloom, David H. 1986. *Public Administration: Understanding Management, Politics, and Law in the Public Sector*. New York: Random House.

Sargent, Alice. 1978. "The Androgynous Blend." *Management Review* 67 (October): 60–65.

Simon, Herbert A. 1973. "Organization Man: Rational or Self-Actualizing." *Public Administration Review*, 33: 346–353.

Simon, Herbert A. 1976. *Administrative Behavior: A Study of Decision-Making Processes in Administrative Organizations*. 3d. ed. New York: The Free Press.

Smith, Michael P. 1976. "Barriers to Organizational Democracy in Public Administration." *Administration and Society* 18: 275–317.

Stewart, Debra W., and G. David Garson. 1983. *Organizational Behavior and Public Management*. New York: Marcel Dekker.

Taylor, Frederick W. 1913. *Principles of Scientific Management*. New York: Harper.

Thompson, James. 1967. *Organizations In Action*. New York: McGraw-Hill.

White, Ralph, and Ronald Lippitt. 1968. "Leader Behavior and Member Reaction in Three Social Climates." In *Group Dynamics: Research and Theory*, eds. Darwin Cartwright and Alvin Zander. New York: Harper & Row.

Chapter 5

ALLOCATING RESOURCES: PLANNING, BUDGETING, AND EVALUATION

Careful allocation of resources under swampy conditions is difficult. It is hard to plan what to do and to implement those plans when conditions are generally uncertain. Nonetheless, administrators must take the larger picture and longer term into account as they allocate scarce resources to various activities of their organizations. No matter how uncertain the environment, it is useful to keep an old Army saying in mind: "Supervisors fight alligators, administrators drain swamps."

Draining swamps is categorically a different kind of activity than fighting alligators. Fighting alligators is likely to be reactive, have a short-time horizon, and seem rather frantic. In contrast, making the swamp a better place in which to live requires a more active stance, longer time frames, and a cooler perspective toward rapid change. Planning, budgeting, and evaluation activities can, if done well, equip the administrator to spend less time fighting the beasts and more time creatively dealing with the total environment.

In the process of becoming more active managers, public administrators must give special attention to several management functions. *Management functions* are those activities that administrators carry out as they implement public policy. Allocation of fiscal and human resources to various tasks is a primary management function. Public agencies usually operate within broad policy guidelines established by their governing bodies and the courts. Administrators use considerable discretion as they turn general policies into organizational goals, specific objectives, and management tasks. Setting and meeting goals involve administrators in several important management activities including planning, budgeting, and evaluation.

Planning is a process by which a scheme is devised to accomplish a given set of goals. Planning requires administrators to translate the mission of the organization into measurable goals and to indicate their choices of the best ways to achieve those goals.

Budgeting is a process whereby resources are allocated among different purposes. Generally, there are too few resources and too many needs. Thus, budgeting allocates scarce resources among competing needs in the expectation that the mix of activities supported will lead to the achievement of agency goals and that the services produced will meet important needs of the community.

Evaluation is a process of assessing the effectiveness of planned activities supported by budgeted resources in achieving stated goals. Evaluation helps administrators find out if and when what they are attempting to do is being accomplished, and if those activities have any positive benefits for the community.

PLANNING BY ADMINISTRATORS

Governmental planning has many forms. Many of us are most familiar with the idea of urban planning (Catanese and Snyder 1979). Urban planning attempts to relate and to shape various aspects of urban settlements such as transportation, land use, air and water quality, housing, and public spaces into an amenable environment for the improvement of the quality of life in cities. Social planning tries to use governmental power to achieve such goals as more equitable distribution of income, equal employment opportunity, reduced unemployment, and a more stable economy. Although social planning is not ideologically popular in the United States and is strongly opposed by many people, since the New Deal of the 1930s all governments in this country have engaged more and more in social planning. Military and defense planning is a major part of the national government's planning efforts. Governmental planning for public capital projects such as roads, highways, sewage treatment plants, irrigation projects, and flood control systems has taken place since or before the founding of the Republic. These examples all involve the use of governmental power to achieve some important political, economic, or social goal. This is program or policy planning.

Planning also refers to internal activities done in a single organization to help it follow the most promising paths toward achievement of its mission and goals. This is *implementation planning* (Graham and Hays 1986). In this sense, planning is an important aid to effective decision making inside the agency. Implementation planning is part of a total set of processes which in the end may lead to attainment of some larger policy goal. For example, a state department of water resources may have the mandate from the state legislature to reduce the consumption of groundwater in rural areas by 20 percent over a ten-year period. The department in conjunction with the governor's office and the state department of lands has produced a ten-year plan for doing this. In the process of implementing this policy plan, the department of water resources also engages in internal planning for the allocation of departmental resources and efforts to the goals and tasks necessary to do its part in attaining the more general policy goal.

Planning helps the organization to be forward looking. It provides schemes and processes which ultimately, if successful, lead to the coordination of efforts of the various subunits of the organization. Planning helps the organization anticipate and shape change. Under swampy conditions, an organization needs to spend considerable effort in studying the environment so it can anticipate some of the important changes taking place and proactively adjust to them. In addition, the organization can purposefully interact with the environment to foster external changes favorable to it.

Steps in the Planning Process

Plans are proposals for the future. Planning is the process whereby proposals for the future are devised and assessed. The classical model of the planning process consists of five interrelated steps (Banfield 1955; Friend and Jessop 1969):

Identification of Needs. The general needs that public agencies meet are typically set out in their constitutions, by the enabling legislation, or in the annual budget bills or expenditure plans enacted by the governing body. Nonetheless, administrators frequently have considerable discretion in seeking out and specifying the precise needs that are to be filled by the actions of their organizations. For example, city managers often have great latitude in devising an economic development plan for their cities.

Specification of Goals and Objectives. The general mission of the organization is translated into several goals and each goal is divided into a number of objectives. Goals are the future state of events that the administrators wish to accomplish in a given time period. In the case of a large urban region's air quality program, the overall goal might be to bring the quality of the region's air into compliance with federally mandated standards within five years. Objectives are the intermediate outcomes that are to be accomplished to reach a goal. Objectives of the air quality plan might be the closing of a smelter or the reduction of the use of private automobiles for commuting.

Development of Alternative Means To Attain Each Goal. Almost any goal may be achieved by more than one means. Managers need to identify several promising ways of reaching a goal and then systematically compare them. A temptation for all managers is to limit the list of alternatives to two or three. It is better for managers to force themselves to make a larger rather than a smaller list of alternatives. This helps prevent missing a potentially useful alternative and provides the manager with backup alternatives in case some do not work well. Furthermore, many managers find that they must develop mixed strategies in which more than one way to accomplish a given goal is attempted at the same time. In an arid area, conservation of water is an important goal. Municipal water providers often must use a combination of approaches to encourage people to conserve water. Such a combination could include efforts to educate water users, rebates and tax incentives for developers and home owners who install water-conserving plumbing, and higher water charges during the summer months to discourage high consumption of water. The majority of the agency's efforts might be invested in development and implementation of a system of seasonal increases in water charges as a means of regulation of water use, but in most communities this option would be supplemented with other approaches as well.

Estimation of the Costs of Each Alternative. Choice among the potential alternatives for implementation usually is based upon some form of *cost analysis.* Sometimes identification of the way to proceed is done on the basis of which alternatives cost the least. A more sophisticated approach makes use of *benefit-cost analysis,* in which all of the benefits and costs of each alternative are systematically compared with those of each other alternative. This approach permits choice of the alternative that promotes more effective use of scarce resources.

Selection of the Most Promising Alternative(s). In a stable world, faithfully carrying out the above four steps would indicate to the decision maker the *best* alternative, in the sense that if it is implemented, it would have the best chance of meeting the stated goals and objectives. In a swampy world, the manager may have to select the *most promising* options in order to be able to spread the risk of failure.

The most promising options are those which offer some prospect of achieving the desired goal. Usually the manager is unable to identify the single best option, but can identify several alternatives which promise to bring the organization close to its desired goal. Thus, managers often must deal with several options. One would want to select the most promising but also keep some contingency options open.

Limits to Conventional Planning

Planning is by definition *rational*. Managers as planners attempt to apply their rationality to making proposals for the future. They hope to make things better. Often their hopes and expectations are dashed on the hard rocks of reality. There are several general reasons why rational planning is limited and why planning often fails.

First, human frailty limits rationality. Herbert Simon (1976) suggested that humans live in a world of "bounded rationality." Human capacity to be fully rational is limited or bounded by three things: values, skills, and knowledge. The values of managers color and bias their capacity to perceive reality and to assess potential impacts of alternative courses of action. The range of personal or collective skills in an organization may be insufficient to sort out options and assess them. Likewise, the knowledge base possessed may be inadequate for completion of the steps required in fully rational planning. Although education, training, and improved management practices may, in part, help overcome these limits, all decision makers are constrained by these limits. They still can systematically set out, review, and select among options, but it is impossible for them to select the best option.

Second, managers are action-oriented persons (Webber 1972). They want to get things done. They are rewarded for specific accomplishments, usually in a short time frame. As a consequence, they tend to live in the present. Planning, however, requires contemplation and a long time frame. Thus, managers are not natural planners and often resist devoting the time and effort needed to do a good job of planning (Berkley 1984).

Third, the world is uncertain. As we have stated before, the external environment changes so rapidly and so unpredictably that the capacity to get a fix on it is severely limited. Planning under these conditions must be fluid. This observation at first seems a contradiction. Planning pursues preferred futures. How can the pursuit of a preferred state of affairs be fluid? It is fluid because of the need to adapt and to adjust plans continuously during their implementation. Thus, plans are best viewed as "strategic guides" rather than fixed paths to the future. Even so, the swampy environment means that most plans will not produce the results originally expected of them.

Fourth, planning is concerned with individual and community values (Bolan 1967; Simon, Smithberg, and Thompson 1950). Plans propose to change the current distribution of public resources. Any recommendation to change the status quo is going to be controversial and raise resistance based upon self-interest. Managers find it difficult both inside their organizations and in dealing with the public to secure basic agreement on goals, alternatives, and which alternatives are most promising. In short, planning always produces conflict.

Strategic Planning

During the 1960s and 1970s, considerable attention was given to a comprehensive approach to planning called *strategic planning* (Mintzberg 1973; Graham and Hays 1986; Steiner 1979). Strategic planning represents an attempt to overcome or at least to account for some of the major limitations of conventional planning in organizations. Table 5.1 compares the major differences between implementation and strategic planning.

Strategic planning provides general guidance for the overall direction and activities of the organization. Implementation planning fleshes out the strategic plan and operationalizes its goals. Strictly speaking, it is not a replacement for more conventional planning approaches but a shell within which implementation planning takes place.

Implementation planning often takes place in a short time frame. Seldom do implementation plans cover more than five years

TABLE 5.1:   Comparison of Implementation and Strategic Planning

Implementation Planning	Strategic Planning
Operational	Strategic shell
Short time frame	Very long time frame
Objectives	Goals
How to do it	What to do
Assigns resources	Assigns priorities
Internal network	External network
Incremental change	Comprehensive change

and most often, implementation plans cover one or two years. In contrast, strategic planning deals in five- to ten-year time frames. The longer time frame of strategic planning helps foster a more long-run perspective among managers and staff alike. It should be noted that even though strategic plans have long time frames, they must be revised regularly to account for environmental changes. Normally, strategic plans are revised every two to three years. Frequent revision is aimed at refreshing the commitment of the organization to its mission, as well as at overcoming the tendency of administrators to get locked on operational concerns.

Strategic planning translates the general mandate and mission of the organization into goals and goal statements. It helps tell the organization and its personnel *what* it should be doing and *why* it is doing it. These goal statements provide the general sense of direction to the agency. The process of setting and continually revising the goals and goal statements provides incentive for administrators to look at the bigger picture and to see unit tasks inside a larger, community-oriented framework. In comparison, implementation planning sets out the specific objectives and tasks to be performed in moving toward the goals. It tells *how* things are to be done.

Implementation planning makes use of the internal network of organizations. It tries to focus the efforts of different units toward a common operational objective. When implementation planning is part of an integrating management approach such as Management by Objectives or Quality Circles, intergroup communication and coordination are enhanced. Although the process of strategic planning fosters internal communication and coordination as well, its main difference from implementation planning is that it links the organization with the external communities and authorities on a regular basis. This external networking not only produces important information about changes in the environment, but it also increases the skill and value base upon which decisions are made. In a sense, it pushes the limits of bounded rationality outward. Strategic planning, in common with participatory management and citizen participation in management, does not fully overcome bounded rationality, but it increases the variety of information and knowledge available to decision makers in their implementation tasks.

There is debate about how incremental or comprehensive policy implementation actually is (Schulman 1975). It is clear that implementation planning is, by its limits, mostly incremental. It focuses on discrete tasks related to specific objectives in short time frames. In contrast, strategic planning mediates incrementalism and produces the capacity to respond more comprehensively to changes and to shape change itself.

Few public organizations actually do much strategic planning; those that do attempt it, appear to do it in name only. Yet, it is clear that if organizations are to adapt better to their swampy environments, they need the kind of marriage of implementation and strategic planning touted by Mintzberg (1973) and Graham and Hays (1986). There are great advantages to strategic approaches to planning, but it remains to be seen if many public organizations can in fact put it successfully into practice.

BUDGETING AS RESOURCE ALLOCATION AND PLANNING

Budgeting is the principal planning effort of many public agencies. It is in the early steps of budget planning that governmental organizations most carefully and fully examine their goals and performance. Further, budgeting secures for a program or an organization the resources needed to continue and perhaps improve its public service activities. Public organizations continue to reform and experiment with attempts to make budgeting more effective.

In some public agencies assessments of the performance of individuals within the agency, the productivity of the organization itself, and the outcomes and impacts of public policy implementation have come to be intimately tied to the allocation of material resources and the budget process. As public managers make more and more use of quantitative measures of employee performance, regular assessments of agency activities, and research-based evaluations of policy impacts, they will use the resulting data sets in the budget process.

Money, along with other agency resources such as human beings, organizational structure, experience, time and technology, support day-to-day activities such as educating our citizens, protecting their property, and providing drinkable water. Since the funds that support public budgets mostly come from involuntary taxes, the size of budgets and what they are used for always are important and often controversial political considerations. Budgets are political documents, budgeting is a political process, and management of budgeting brings administration and pressure-group politics face to face (Wildavsky 1984; Shuman 1984).

Three Views of the Budget

Public budgets may be characterized as *records* of community values, as *plans* laying out goals and resource allocations for a given time period, and as management *tools*. All three views are useful and together they suggest why so much attention is paid to budgeting by chief administrative officers such as mayors, school district superintendents, city managers, governors, and the president.

Record of the Political Process. The final, adopted version of a budget represents the results of months and at times years of political negotiation, compromise, and logrolling. The appropriations among competing interests and demands represented in the final budget and later supplemental appropriations are a summary tally of the winners and losers in the political processes. In this sense, an annual municipal budget is a formal statement of the city's current public policy values and priorities. Since budgets are not made completely in a given year but represent the accumulation of incremental changes made to the past decisions of many years, a budget is a good historical record of the overall values of the local polity.

Working plan. The budget documents, especially in the early stages of preparation and review, are working plans of proposed allocations of resources and of promised performances. Agencies or departments typically are asked by the executive to submit their budget plans in advance of the actual formal consideration of the budget document. In this process, administrators lay out "wish lists" of things they would like to do and goals they would like to accomplish. They must indicate what each task will cost. Often, they must document both the need for proposed levels of services and expected achievements.

Levels of budgetary sophistication and budget preparation practices vary among governmental jurisdictions, but at times, budget preparation puts administrators into a classical planning mode. In this mode, administrators as planners develop their proposed budgets, set out goals, arrange these goals in priority, select ways to achieve these goals, indicate resources needed to reach them, and promise levels of performance.

Budget preparation frequently is much less complete and smooth than is suggested above. Furthermore, the plans made by the administrators often are not part of their written budget proposals. Nonetheless, even in relatively small public organizations, administrators do tie budget preparation and organizational planning together. In large cities, most states, and the national government, administrators do a considerable amount of organizational planning as part of the budget process.

Management Tool. Chief executive officers—mayors, city managers, governors, and presidents—try to use the budget-making process as a tool to influence and control administrative agencies and departments. They set the broad guidelines and constraints to which they hope the administrators and agencies will adhere. Insofar as the executive can direct the budget-planning activities and resist changes to the executive budget, budgeting is a means of exercising some degree of central control over agencies and departments. Executives try to constrain the resource-hunting forays of administrators into the legislative processes through requirements of central clearance of proposed changes and new requests. Further, the chief executive usually presents a completed budget plan to the council or legislature with a statement of executive goals, limits, and principles. Many presidents, governors, mayors, and city managers are surprised at the extent to which departments and agencies successfully resist central control in the budget process. Many a reformer has seen dreams of centralized fiscal management dashed upon the realities of the extent to which the budget process is in the hands of administrators, legislators, and interest groups composing the Iron Triangle.

The Budget Process

Budgets are implemented or executed in time periods called *fiscal years*. The fiscal year (FY) should not be confused with the ordinary calendar year which runs from January 1 through December 31. The typical state or local government's fiscal year is July 1 through June 30. The national government's fiscal year currently is October 1 through September 30. In a given fiscal year, administrators typically work on several steps of the budget process for different years at the same time.

Despite its complexity and variety, the budget cycle consists of five basic steps: (1) research and data base management, which provides the basic information used by budget planners; (2) preparation of a draft or proposed budget; (3) submission and adoption, which translates the proposed budget plan into policy; (4) implementation, which turns the budget appropriations into services; and (5) evaluation, including audit and policy assessment.

Budgeting is continuous, and each of the five steps overlap. Further, in most places, administrators work on two or three year's budget plans at the same time. The overlapping stages and long lead time not only make the job difficult for administrators in handling two or three budgets at a time, but bring them back into continuous contacts with the other participants of the budget-making process. Furthermore, the role and stance of a given organization's administrators change in the different stages of the budget cycle. This may be illustrated by more detailed consideration of budgeting in a municipal setting.

Research and Data Base Development. All budgets are built upon the budgets of past years. The changes from one year to the next are seldom so great that past budget experience is lost. Even with the past as a guide and as a base for future budgets, a certain amount of new information and knowledge is needed in subsequent years if there is to be any sort of real budget planning.

Local administrators normally estimate needs and proposed expenditures *before* they recommend appropriate tax increases (if needed). In larger cities, most states, and the national government, estimation of the upcoming fiscal year's revenues is a key preparatory step. In a large city, the estimate of revenues may reflect the combined efforts of the finance or budget director, the city manager's office, and the planning department. These estimates of revenues from various sources are sometimes based upon demographic and economic forecasts rather than on straight-line projections of past revenues. At best, however, these estimates are rough guides and frequently are incorrect.

Preparation. Budget preparation begins with the establishment of general guidelines by the chief executive. Each department is expected to stay within these guidelines. A department begins its internal preparation with an assessment of policy and program needs. The current fiscal year's budget is generally the *base* and requests from each unit ask for some increment above the amount needed to continue the current year's operations. Based upon these assessments, departmental administrators develop proposed budget plans and supporting documentation. In small towns and cities, these estimates may be informal, but in larger cities, the budget documents may be rather large and elaborate. In larger jurisdictions, this step may include scenarios relating to different levels of available revenues and allocations, as well as specific indications of the promises being made by that department in terms of service and performance levels.

The departmental proposals are reviewed next by the central administration. This is a period of intense negotiation between the department heads and the chief executive. The department budget proposals are modified and compiled into a single budget document by the budget director. Frequently the draft of the executive budget is distributed to department heads for review and comment before a formal budget proposal is revised and prepared for distribution to the city council.

Adoption. The city council members already will have information about the proposed executive budget *before* it is formally transmitted to them by the chief executive officer. Departmental administrators often already will have begun their appeal for support or additional increments or restoration of cuts before completion of the budget preparation. Clientele or support groups also will have got into the act. Council members are often aggressive participants in the preparation stage and usually are informed about departmental proposals by the time the formal executive budget is presented to them.

Nonetheless, formal council consideration of the budget begins *after* presentation of the executive budget. The council may, and usually does, modify, the proposed budget. Political negotiations continue with the chief executive trying to defend and protect the proposed budget and the council challenging it. The council holds public hearings, receives public comment, questions administrators, and makes additional changes in the budget, sometimes radically changing it. During this time, departments and interest group allies often are able to secure changes in the budget. These changes may be with or without the blessing of the mayor or city manager. Although the mayor or city manager may try to enforce central control over the budget, departments and interest groups often can secure changes even in the face of opposition from the chief executive. Finally, at a public meeting, the council adopts the modified budget.

Implementation of the Budget. The budget is implemented by administrators as they attempt to manage their organizations in such a manner as to reach the objectives set out in their implementation plans. This often requires modification of the original budget allocations and changes in proposed activities and services as the organizations adapt to environmental changes. During the fiscal year in which the budget is implemented, the council often is asked to make supplemental allocations upon recommendation of the executive, assuming revenues are available. If fiscal conditions are tight, departmental administrators may be required to make reductions to bring expenditures into line with revenues. In any case, the budget implementation step also is a political process in which administrators continually struggle to protect their organizations and their basic budget allotments.

Audit and Assessment. A formal financial audit usually is required by state law. It consists of review of the accounting records made during the implementation of the budget. The completed audit verifies that the financial transactions conducted by the city were done according to legal requirements and followed generally accepted accounting practices. It typically also testifies to the accuracy of the records and financial reports by stating that they present "fairly" the financial position of the city (Rousmainiere 1979). In past decades, this was the primary form of assessment of the use of budget resources for local governments. Today, in some governmental jurisdictions, additional assessments of performance are made. The performance audit looks more closely at how well the agency met its goals, objectives, and promised performance level. These assessments provide information that is fed into the next budget cycle. This also is a policy assessment stage that helps tie a budget cycle into another by providing information for the data bases used in the future. As part of the next cycle's research effort, the assessment of past performance provides a feedback loop and assists managers in shaping and adapting to change.

The steps of the budget cycle resemble planning. This is particularly true of the portions of the activities that engage administrators. This point is not lost on many managers. In some organizations, research and preparation for the annual budget starts well in advance of the announcement of principles and guidelines by the chief executive. The more sophisticated the management approach of an administrator or an organization, the more the budgeting exercise is used for administrative policy planning.

Budget Reform: Search for Planning in Budgetary Systems

Major attempts to reform budgeting in the United States started at the beginning of the Republic, but this century has been notable for attempts to alter budget forms and practices to improve the managerial aspects of the budget process. We will discuss only a few such efforts here. Students who wish to pursue more complete discussion of budget reform might want to consult Burkhead, *Governmental Budgeting* (1956), Lee and Johnson, *Public Budgeting Systems* (1983), and Schick "The Road to PPB: The Stages of Budget Reform" (1966) for excellent interpretations of budget reforms.

Budgeting as planning has high demands for information. Administrators use two kinds of information in budgeting: resource data and program data (Lee and Johnson 1983). *Resource data* refer to information regarding inputs (resources) such as money, equipment, and human effort used in producing services. *Program data* refer to what the organization does and the accomplishment of those activities. Planning requires that both kinds of information must be considered in combination. Neither kind of data alone will answer the questions posed in a systematic planning process. If budgeting is to assist managers in making good planning decisions and to help adjust to a changing environment, then the budgetary system must produce and use both kinds of data. As Lee and Johnson (1983) suggest, much of the change in budgetary practices and forms may be viewed as an attempt to develop program data and to link it with resource data.

There are two general kinds of budgets and supporting systems in use today: line item and performance/program. A third system, zero base budgeting, is a variation of the performance/program approach and is used in local governments. They deal with resource and program data differently, and each provides a different environment for budgeting.

Line Item Budget Systems. The line item budget is the most common form used today. Even jurisdictions that use a version of performance/program budgeting systems usually use line item information somewhere in their budget-making processes.

The conventional line item budget details expenditures of each department by objective of expenditure and amount. There is a "budget line" for each expenditure item such as every salaried position, wages, travel, long-distance telephone calls, expendable materials, and energy costs. Line item listings are likely to be very detailed and fill page after page with neat columns of expenditure items, their proposed number, and the resulting expenditure amount.

Line item budgets were originally developed so that the chief administrator and the legislature could get a detailed set of fiscal information for each department or agency. The idea was to increase administrative and legislative oversight and review of draft budgets. The mountains of detail contained in contemporary line item budgets make oversight a tedious task and often lead to nit-picking about details. Line item budgets have, however, fostered universal use of financial audit as a major accountability mechanism.

Line item budgets focus attention on the allocation of resources to very specific purposes. They permit the auditor, legislator, or executive to know for what specific items departments and agencies spend funds. In contrast to the detailed information provided about specific uses of resources, line item budgets provide little, if any, information about the overall accomplishments of the departments supported by the resources. They do not provide any information about the relationships among various expenditures or what happens as a result of expenditures. Reformers long have criticized the line item approach to budgeting for encouraging incrementalism in budgeting and for failing to promote the development of information useful in program planning (Lee and Johnson 1983).

Incrementalism in budgeting is the process whereby this year's appropriations become the *base* for next year's budget. In the preparation of their budget proposals, departments and agencies tend to take what they currently have as given and ask for some additional increment above it for the next fiscal year.

By the 1930s, it became clear that traditional budget formats and practices did not make sense to those administrators interested in program planning and more central control of budgeting. (See Caiden 1987 for a discussion of the executive budget.) The national, state, and most local budgets were not rational, comprehensive documents that reflected the overall annual plans of the jurisdiction but were rather a compilation of hundreds and thousands of individual requests and allocations to specific units to do specific tasks. As political objects, the budget and the budget process were elegant summaries of interest group-agency-legislative interaction with the agency playing the key role of protector of the public budgetary base of their operations (Wildavsky 1984; Shuman 1984). As Wildavsky has shown, public agencies tend to treat last year's budget as the "base" upon which to ask for this year's increase. Thus, the agency tries to protect this base in negotiations with the legislature regarding increases or cuts.

Program/Performance Budgeting. Although some authors discuss program and performance budgeting separately (Turnbull 1981), they are variations on a theme (Lee and Johnson 1983) and will be treated as one approach here. Support for programmatic approaches to budgeting in the 1930s and 1940s grew out of the need to permit managers more flexibility in allocating resources to organizational activities (Burkhead 1956). At the national level, the 1949 Hoover Commission report stressed the advantages of the "performance" budget and recommended that it be adopted throughout the national government (Commission on the Organization of the Executive Branch of the Government 1949). A sophisticated version of program/performance based budgeting called Planning Programming Budgeting Systems (PPBS) was introduced at the national level in the 1960s. Although PPBS lasted only a few years at the national level, a few states and some local governments now use some form of program budgeting.

Program budgeting differs from line item budgeting in three important ways: (1) more attention is given to specification of program goals and objectives; (2) funds are distributed on the basis of program results; (3) departments are expected to demonstrate quantitatively the expected achievements at different levels of funding.

Administrators prepare program budgets differently from line item budgets. Instead of proposing budgets on the basis of line items, managers preparing program budgets usually do the following:

1. Define the major programs of the organization. In a municipal police department, these might be traffic control, crime prevention and control, investigation, internal affairs, training, and community relations.

2. Specify a set of goals and objectives for each program and develop measurements for each objective. A goal of the police crime prevention and control program is to prevent crimes by patrol of residential neighborhoods. Typical objectives might be to decrease crimes against person by 3 percent, reduce the number of persons injured in the commission of crimes by 7 percent, and to decrease average response time by one minute. A measure for the first objective, the decrease in the number of crimes against person, probably would be the number of different kinds of crimes reported per 1,000 population.

3. Identify the various inputs (resources) to be used to produce the desired results. Using the program structure and the measurement systems, the police budget analysts then prepare a budget that shows what level of service the department proposes for each program and the resources required to support these programs.

In subsequent years, the departmental administrators, chief executive of the city, the council, and even the public can tell if the department is meeting its objectives. This information is part of the evaluation of departmental performance and ties planning, budgeting, and evaluation together.

Program budgeting provides a better overview of objectives and expenditures, how they relate to each other, and how cost-effective different components of total agency effort may be. Nonetheless, PPBS did not last long in the national government and is seldom found in pure form in other governments. Why? Three very strong reasons. First, it flies in the face of incrementalism and incrementalism is the rule of the established politics of the budget process. Second, it is a complex, cumbersome process that requires considerable time and effort be spent on development of measures of benefits and costs, goal setting, and priority setting. Third, it makes it clear which programs are cost-effective; and there are many favorite programs supported by agencies, interests, and legislators that are not cost-effective.

Zero Base Budgeting. Zero base budgeting (ZBB) is a variation of program/performance budgeting. Although seldom used in pure form, variants are used in many city-manager systems. Zero base budgeting was developed in the private sector (Pyhrr 1977), briefly used by the U. S. Department of Agriculture in 1964, adopted by several states including Georgia, and implemented at the national level in the Carter administration in 1977.

ZBB is defined as:

A budgeting technique that generally attempts to analyze budget requests without an implicit commitment to sustaining past levels of funding. Under this system, programs and activities are organized and budgeted in a detailed plan that focuses review, evaluation, and analysis on all proposed operations— rather than on increases above current levels of operation, as in incremental budgeting. Programs and activities are analyzed in terms of successively increasing levels of performance and funding, starting from zero, and then evaluated and ranked in priority order. The purpose is to determine the level, if any, at which each program or activity should be conducted. (General Accounting Office, 1979).

According to Berkley (1984), the ZBB approach has three steps:

1. *Indentification of decision units.* In this first step, the organization's activities are clustered into separate decision units. In a university, such units could be academic departments, research centers, or administrative offices. The key is that all of the activities of the organization must be assigned to some decision unit.

2. *Preparation of decision packages.* Each decision unit prepares budget proposals for that unit called "decision packages." All of the unit's activities and programs could operate at various levels depending on how fully they are funded. The administrators of each unit develop a plan that shows several different gradations of activities, each with its own quantity of resources and outputs. These program and resource data

form the decision package for a given level of activity. The different decision packages collectively may range from zero to some very high level and the differences between them show the relative impacts on programs of various levels of funding.

3. *Ranking decision packages.* Once the organization has prepared its decision packages, it ranks them in order of its priorities. After the originating unit does its rankings, the decision packages are passed up to the administrative level above it. If the original unit was an academic department, then the dean's office would be the next level. Here the decision packages of one unit compete with those of another and all are reranked. They then go to the next levels—academic vice president, president, and board of regents—where they are combined with all other decision packages and reranked at each level. ZBB principles suggest that in each successive reranking decision makers consider how well the decision package fits into the larger scope of priorities at that level. Often, decision packages are modified or combined as they pass through the levels of review and reranking. In the end, the continual reuse of program and resource information is supposed to increase the rationality of the budget preparation, review, and compilations processes.

ZBB is very flexible and permits adjustments to changing conditions because it is based on program evaluation (Pyhrr 1977). Nonetheless, it did not work well in the national government and was abandoned by the Reagan administration in 1981. Its critics find that ZBB requires excessive effort in research and budget preparation, creates mountains of paperwork (Hammond and Knott, 1980), does not actually overcome incrementalism (Lauth 1978), and focuses too narrowly on the process of ranking decision packages to the detriment of considering outside influences (Mikesell 1982).

ZBB is similar to program/performance budgeting in three important ways. First, they both stress goal setting and results. Second, they cluster expenditures into program or activity groups. Third, they require quantitative measures of outcomes. ZBB is best seen as a variation of the general program/performance approach to budgeting in which the development of information for program planning plays such an important role.

Formal program budgeting is dead at the national level, rarely used in the states, and more frequently used in cities. Although it provides the chief executive with considerable control over budgeting, program budgeting is hard to do and cumbersome. Despite its limits and failures, some of its principles and practices are part of budgeting and program evaluation. The effort to provide program information through the identification and measurement of objectives continues. There is much more emphasis at all levels of government on the use of program information in budget preparation and adoption.

EVALUATION

Information about the performance of organizations and the impacts of their programs is crucial to administrators coping with the uncertainty of life in the swamp. Adjustment to rapidly changing conditions requires a steady diet of information about how well things are going. Evaluation studies increasingly are a major source of needed information about the relationship between organizations and their uncertain, ever-changing environment.

Performance-oriented budgeting encourages public administrators to pay attention to the consequences of how their organizations use resources. Although PPBS and ZBB approaches to budgeting now are seldom practiced in their pure forms, many local governments use some variant of them. Even in organizations which have moved away from performance-based budgeting, there continues to be considerable emphasis upon evaluation of organization and program performance. The complexities of pure performance-based budgeting generally have led to more streamlined practices, but a lasting contribution of PPBS and ZBB is the continued development and use of evaluation information in the planning and allocation activities of many public organizations.

Budget reform is just one of the roots of evaluation research. Applied research for evaluation of the performance of public organizations and programs dates at least from the 1940s, but the social reform programs of the 1960s spawned widespread evaluation research as social scientists renewed their interest in topics such as crime, poverty, education, and urban development. Practicing public administrators were less quick to move toward use of evaluation research for assessment of their organizations and programs. By the mid-1970s, however, efforts to promote the use of *evaluation research* by public administrators were found at all levels of American government (Hatry, et al. 1973; General Accounting Office 1976; Fukahera 1977).

What is evaluation research? It is similar to but different from ordinary "hypothesis testing" social inquiry. In hypothesis testing research, the inquiry is directed toward testing a set of empirical propositions to see if they are valid. The validation process usually leads to the development of a theory that explains social phenomena. Evaluation research is applied research that uses theory, research design, and methods to provide evaluation information about the performance of organizations and their programs. It may lead to refinement of social theory, but its main purpose is to aid administrators in their assessment of how well their organizations and programs are working.

Program Evaluation

Program evaluation is the evaluation research conducted to assess the programs implemented by public organizations. Program evaluation in the United States probably dates from early in this century but is only now coming into common practice. Public administrators are learning that they need to know more about the consequences of the use of organization resources in order to increase their effectiveness. Program evaluation provides part of the feedback that encourages organizations to adjust to a changing, uncertain environment.

Major Purposes of Program Evaluation. Program evaluation has three major purposes. First, it provides information about the degree to which a program is actually reaching its objectives. Second, it informs administrators and other policymakers about the unintended consequences of implementation of the program. Often, programs have negative or positive consequences that are not anticipated. If the unintended consequences are harmful and outweigh the positive results of the achievement of the nominal objectives of the program, then policymakers have reason to alter or abolish the program. Third, it often provides information about the level of public satisfaction with the outcomes of the program and the degree of public support for the program. This is vital information in the politically charged environment of most programs.

Carefully prepared program evaluations often provide administrators with useful information. On the other hand, program evaluations are frequently disregarded by the very administrators and organizations for which they are prepared. This suggests that there are some serious problems with program evaluations.

Problems with Program Evaluation. Like most innovations, the actual practice of program evaluation differs from theoretical expectations about it. Major problems may be clustered into three groups of related issues. First, program evaluations often are marked by tensions between the evaluators and the administrators of the programs. Second, measurement of program outcomes and impacts is very difficult. Third, program evaluations may not produce much usable information.

Program evaluation may be done by members of the organization, but most frequently it is done by outsiders. This may produce a kind of doctor-patient relationship in which the evaluator treats the organization and its administrators as "sick" and in need of "therapy" (Archebald 1970). In this situation, little trust develops between the evaluator and those evaluated. The resulting tension not only weakens the evaluation itself, but in the long run, reduces the probability that the organization will make use of the recommendations of the evaluation report. Even if the evaluator develops a more positive relationship with the organization and its members, evaluation reports that pose serious questions and provide negative feedback are viewed with some suspicion by administrators.

A very serious issue for program evaluation is the extent to which the evaluation actually measures and assesses the performance of an organization and program. There are two key aspects of this problem that plague evaluators. First, can the effects of the "treatment" (the program) be assessed separately from all of the other factors that may have contributed to the actual outcomes? Good research design and use of appropriate statistical tools, especially time series analysis, enhance the possibility of successfully isolating the effects of the program, but it is frequently very difficult to tell if the treatment is producing positive results. Second, measurement of outcomes and impacts is very difficult. Inputs such as units of resources—money, time, energy—used to implement the program are relatively easy to measure, but outcomes and impacts, which are the consequences of the program for the external environment, are much more difficult to measure.

Using a traffic control program as an illustration, we can demonstrate some of the key problems with measuring and assessing the outcomes and impacts of public programs.

Outputs might include the number of hours of patrol, the number of officers on foot at intersections regulating traffic flow, and the number of warnings or citations issued. All of these items are accepted "measures" of traffic control outputs, but do they measure well the consequences of the program? Probably not. Let us turn to "outcomes." A major outcome of good traffic control is more orderly traffic flow over streets and freeways. Yet, how much of the orderly or disorderly flow of traffic on the freeway is attributable to police efforts and how much to other factors such as mechanical breakdowns and weather? As much as the police chief would like to take credit for those few mornings when the freeways flow well, the department usually has very little data to show the consequences of traffic control on flow. Things get even more indistinct when we turn to *impacts.* Impacts are the long-term social consequences of public programs. Impacts may be intended or unintended. They also may be positive or negative. An intended, positive impact of traffic control is possible reduction in the number of fatalities resulting from traffic accidents. Fatalities in automobile accidents are likely to result from unsafe vehicles, careless driving, poor weather conditions, or drunk drivers. Insofar as the outcome of more orderly traffic flow contributes to safer driving and fewer chances for vehicles to collide, then it could contribute to the impact of reduced fatalities. Other examples of intended impacts upon the more general improved condition of life related to traffic control include energy savings and cleaner air. Unfortunately for the police, we have little capacity to show the impact of traffic control on these things.

The current quantity and quality of the feedback available to most organizations is insufficient. That is, we cannot measure productivity well enough to provide hard information to the managers and staff who produce the goods and services. Traditional measures such as numbers of persons on patrol, response time, and number of accidents are at best indirect and at worst, measures of the use of resources rather than real outputs, outcomes, and impacts. This issue is further complicated because many of the things police and other public agencies perform do not lend themselves well to unit measurement. Much of the effort of the police officer and the social worker is given to handling domestic relations. Measuring such things as stopping a quarrel or keeping a family together except in terms of frequency of occurrence is very difficult.

Usefulness of Program Evaluations. Few governmental officials make direct use of evaluation research. There are a number of reasons for this. First, much evaluation research is done by academicians and addresses problems in such a way that the results often are not useful to administrators and other policymakers (Lindblom and Cohen 1979). Second, life in the swamp with its pressure for survival does not entice administrators to make careful use of evaluation reports (Daily 1983). Third, the findings of evaluation studies often are threatening and harsh, at least in the eyes of the administrators (Weiss 1982; Greer and Greer 1982).

On the positive side, there is more emphasis on program evaluation than ever before. Further, as Carol Weiss (1977) argues, the very act of conducting an evaluation is important in itself to the organization. The process of conducting the research, while it may be unnerving, promotes a sense of introspection in the organization. Members of the organization refresh their concern with program goals and become concerned with how well things are going. Thus, while the organization may not formally respond to the recommendations of the evaluation report, it may alter its behavior in response to being studied.

All in all, is program evaluation worth the effort? This is the kind of question that led to the rapid decline of PPBS and ZBB. The experience appears to be more mixed with regard to program evaluation. A lot of program evaluation is not done well. Only a small fraction of program evaluation has found its way back into the policy stream and organizational practice. Nonetheless, there is some hope. Localities that use modified forms of program budgeting often utilize simple program evaluation studies to provide information for use in budgeting. Some programs have regular assessments mandated by governing bodies. Impact statements, most often required for assessing environmental consequences, are widely used. Some localities and states have "sunsetting" provisions which make use of program evaluations. Sunset laws require automatic review of agencies and programs by the legislature. These laws force assessment of on-going programs by both legislators and administrators and encourage use of program evaluations.

Although program evaluations are seldom fully utilized by administrators and others, when they are, they provide information useful in adjusting organizations to a changing environment.

Productivity and Assessment of Employee Performance

Assessment of employees' performance provides additional evaluation information that public administrators find useful in their efforts to be more effective in the use of resources. It is probably true that, as in the case of program evaluation, few organizations make full use of data gathered in evaluation of employees. Nonetheless, some do. Cutback management provides special incentives to make assessment of employee performance a normal part of planning and budgeting. Reduction of resources and in the workforce make administrators increasingly interested in the work load and productivity of employees.

Assessing Employee Performance. The efficiency of converting inputs into usable outputs and desirable outcomes and impacts depends a great deal upon employee effectiveness. As argued in our discussion of participatory management, quality circles and MBO, effective management depends largely upon healthy, satisfied employees. It is not enough to rely upon good organization and management practices. Contemporary organizational life requires some kind of systematic assessment of employee effectiveness for a variety of reasons: program evaluation, rewarding staff, demonstrating good use of material resources, and meeting collective bargaining constraints (Cayer 1986; Hyde 1982).

Many jurisdictions make use of regular assessments of employees by their immediate supervisors. Elaborate sets of criteria and check off lists have been devised to aid the supervisor in this onerous task. Typically, the supervisor rates each employee by such criteria as work habits, interpersonal skills, technical skills, and efforts to improve performance.

Often the rating sheet is shared with the employee who is asked to indicate acceptance or disagreement with the assessment by adding comments and signing the document. Infrequently, employees are required to self-assess their performance and compare this with that of the supervisor. In a minority of systems, there is peer evaluation which feeds into the supervisors assessment. In a very few organizations, the subordinate also rates the supervisor.

No matter how carefully done, there are serious problems with even the most progressive assessment system (Nalbandian 1981; McGregor 1957). The first is counterintuitive: most supervisors rank their employees higher than their performance warrants (Berkley 1984). This is probably due to their desire to protect their units and their own jobs. The opposite also happens, but not as frequently as overrating. Second, the annual assessment period is very upsetting to all and even those employees who do well show strain and tend to be dysfunctional for a time. Third, assessments tend to become routine and the basic data suspect as all parties learn to beat the system.

The most important issue, however, is germane to all forms of assessment. Employee evaluation is essentially subjective and no matter how rigorous the criteria and methodology, the final judgment is just that: a subjective judgment of another person. This is why good organizational health and participatory management are so important. Unless there is considerable trust and acceptance on the part of the subordinates, no employee evaluation system will work.

Organizational Performance

The assessment of whole organizations is also uncertain. Even the use of MBO and performance budgeting still focuses assessments of organizations on degrees of achievement of specified goals. It sounds sensible to say that we should judge organizations in terms of goal attainment. This assumes that the goals are known, reachable, agreed upon, and measurable. Should a prison be assessed in terms of how many prisoners it handles per month, the number of persons it passes through, the number of prisoners rehabilitated, the occurrence of recidivism in its ex-inmates, the lack of riots, or by what criteria? Or what about libraries? How can we accurately measure goal achievement? By such measures as number of books circulated, number of special reading classes for the young, impact on literacy, quality of the collection, number of fines levied, books lost or recovered?

Notice that we are now back with one of the most serious problems with deciding what to plan and program for. What are some good measures of outputs, outcomes, and impacts? At this time, there is little agreement on measures. Mostly, agencies (and legislatures) opt for indicators of input measures such as number of dollars expended, gallons of fuel used, and numbers of faculty available to teach. Sometimes output measures such as cases handled, books circulated, citations issued, and gallons of water delivered are used in planning, budgeting, and assessment.

One of the more positive spin-offs of programmed budgeting and productivity assessments has been the increased awareness of the public, elected officials, interest groups, and managers to the issues of performance assessments and the need for more objective, valid measures and assessment systems. One can argue that much of the program evaluation and policy analysis done in the past twenty-five years has been flawed, but an equal argument can be made that a new subdiscipline of public administration is developing. There is little question that the surveys of community satisfaction, program analysis, and cost-effectiveness studies done for some programs and in some governmental agencies have served the public well. The public is becoming more aware and better informed about the performance of public agencies. Officials are more responsive and more sensitive to community values. Managers pay more attention to final outcomes. Organizations strive a bit harder for better internal and external feedback.

It is important to remember that we are at the beginning of the development of systematic assessment rather than at some mature point. There is still much to be done in the study and the practice of program evaluation and policy assessment. Among the most important things is to increase use of time series analysis to show better the long term successes and failures of policies. A considerable amount of longitudinal work has been done in applied science and engineering, but little work has been done in the social sciences, especially public administration.

The balance sheet on how well organizations develop and make use of evaluation information is not yet closed. As suggested several times, public administrators need considerable evaluation information to perform well in the swamp. Public administration practice is getting better at developing the needed information and some progress is being made in putting it to use. In the next chapter, we examine the effectiveness of organizational response to environmental change and uncertainty. The rate of successful adjustment is an open question, but the processes of planning, budgeting, and evaluation assist organizations in developing capacity to handle change.

REFERENCES

Archebald, K. A. 1970. "Alternative Orientations to Social Science Utilization." *Social Science Informant*, 9: 7–35.

Banfield, Edward C. 1955. "Notes on a Conceptual Scheme." In *Politics, Planning, and the Public Interest*, eds. Martin Meyerson and Edward C. Banfield. Glencoe, Ill.: Free Press. 303–29.

Berkley, George E. 1984. *The Craft of Public Administration*. 4th ed. Boston: Allyn & Bacon.

Bolan, Richard S. 1967. "Emerging Views of Planning." *Journal of the American Institute of Planners*, 33: 233–245.

Burkhead, Jesse. 1956. *Governmental Budgeting*. New York: Wiley.

Caiden, Naomi. 1987. "Paradox, Ambiguity, and Enigma: The Strange Case of the Executive Budget and the United States Constitution." *Public Administration Review*, 47: 84–92.

Catanese, Anthony J., and James C. Snyder, eds. 1979. *Introduction to Urban Planning*. New York: McGraw-Hill.

Cayer, N. Joseph. 1986. *Public Personnel Administration in the United States*. 2d ed. New York: St. Martin's Press.

The Commission on Organization of the Executive Branch of the Government 1949. *Budgeting and Accounting*. Washington, D.C.: U. S. Government Printing Office. Referenced in Robert D. Lee, Jr. and Ronald W. Johnson. 1983. *Public Budgeting Systems*. 3d ed. Baltimore: University Park Press.

Daily, J. H. 1983. "Overcoming Obstacles to Program Evaluation in Local Government." *Policy Studies Journal*, 12: 287–294.

Friend, J. K., and W. N. Jessop. 1969. *Local Government and Strategic Choice*. London: Tavistock.

Fukahera, Rackham S. 1977. "Productivity Improvement in Cities." *1977 Municipal Yearbook*. Washington, D.C.: International City Management Association.

General Accounting Office. 1976. *Evaluation and Analysis to Support Decision-Making*, PAD-75.9, September 1.

General Accounting Office. 1979. *Streamlining Zero-Base Budgeting Will Benefit Decision Making*. Washington: U. S. Government Printing Office.

Graham, Cole Blease, Jr., and Steven W. Hays. 1986. *Managing the Public Organization*. Washington, D.C.: CQ Press.

Greer, T. V., and J. G. Greer. 1982. "Problems in Evaluating Costs and Benefits of Social Programs." *Public Administration Review*, 42: 151–156.

Hammond, Thomas, and Jack Knott. 1980. *A Zero-Based Look at Zero-Base Budgeting.* New Brunswick, N.J.: Transaction Books.

Hatry, Harry P., et al. 1973. *Practical Program Evaluation for State and Local Government Officials.* Washington, D.C.: Urban Institute.

Hyde, Albert C. 1982. "Performance Appraisal in the Post-Reagan Era." *Public Personnel Management,* 11: 294–305.

International City Management Association (ICMA). 1981. *Management Policies in Local Government Finance.* Washington, D.C.: ICMA.

Lauth, Thomas P. 1978. "Zero-Base Budgeting in Georgia State Government: Myth and Reality." *Public Administration Review,* 38: 420–430.

Lee, Robert D., Jr., and Ronald W. Johnson. 1983. *Public Budgeting Systems.* 3d ed. Baltimore: University Park Press.

Lindblom, Charles E. 1959. "The Science of Muddling Through." *Public Administration Review,* 19: 79–88.

Lindblom, Charles E., and David K. Cohen. 1979. *Usable Knowledge: Social Science and Social Problem Solving.* New Haven: Yale University Press.

McGregor, Douglas. 1957. "An Uneasy Look at Performance Appraisal." *Harvard Business Review,* 35: 89–94.

Mikesell, John L. 1982. "Governmental Decisions in Budgeting and Taxation: The Economic Logic." *Public Administration Review,* 38: 511–513.

Mintzberg, Henry. 1973. *The Nature of Managerial Work.* New York: Harper & Row.

Nachez, Peter B., and Irwin C. Bupp. 1973. "Policy and Priority in the Budgetary Process." *American Political Science Review,* 67: 951–963.

Nalbandian, John. 1981. "Performance Appraisal: If Only People Were Not Involved." *Public Administration Review,* 41: 392–396.

Pyhrr, Peter A. 1977. "The Zero-Base Approach to Government Budgeting." *Public Administration Review,* 37: 1–8.

Rousmainiere, Peter F., ed. 1979. *Local Government Auditing, A Manual for Public Officials.* New York: Council on Municipal Affairs.

Sarant, Peter C. 1978. *Zero-Base Budgeting in the Public Sector: A Pragmatic Approach.* Reading, Mass.: Wiley.

Schick, Allen. 1966. "The Road to PPB: The Stages of Budget Reform." *Public Administration Review,* 26: 243–58.

Schulman, Paul R. 1975. "Nonincremental Policy Making: Notes Toward an Alternative Paradigm." *American Political Science Review.* 69: 1354–1370.

Shuman, Howard E. 1984. *Politics and the Budget: The Struggle Between the President and Congress.* Englewood Cliffs, N.J.: Prentice-Hall.

Simon, Herbert A. 1976. *Administrative Behavior: A Study of Decision-Making Processes in Administrative Organizations.* 3d ed. New York: The Free Press.

Simon, H. A., D. W. Smithberg, and V. A. Thompson. 1950. *Public Administration.* New York: Knopf.

Steiner, G. A. 1979. *Strategic Planning: What Every Manager Must Know.* New York: Free Press.

Straussman, Jeffrey D. 1985. *Public Administration.* New York: Holt.

Turnbull, Augustus B. III. 1981. "The Budgetary Process and Decision Making in Public Agencies." Chapter nine in *Contemporary Public Administration*, eds. Thomas Vocino and Jack Rabin, 231–239. New York: Harcourt.

Webber, Ron A. 1972. *Time and Management*, 160–61. New York: Van Nostrand.

Weiss, Carol H. 1977. "Research for Policy's Sake: The Enlightenment Function of Social Research." *Policy Analysis*, 3: 532–545.

Weiss, Carol H. 1982. "Measuring the Use of Evaluation." *Evaluation Studies Review Annual*, 7: 129–145.

Wildavsky, Aaron. 1984. *The Politics of the Budgetary Process.* 4th ed. Boston: Little, Brown.

Chapter 6

RESPONDING TO CHANGE: IMPROVING SUPPORT AND PERFORMANCE

Public administrators face new challenges on a daily basis. Mark Twain is reputed to have said, "History is just one damn thing after another." Not all new things are damnable, but it often seems that way to the hard-pressed director of corrections, city manager, or liaison officer for the Department of State. Budget reductions, reductions in force, public criticism, and lack of support from elected officials plague managers at all levels. Other changes, especially those in technology, management techniques, and employee skills offer managers opportunities for improving the overall performance of their organizations.

The fluid environment produces a sense of urgency and uncertainty among managers. Life in the swamp is increasingly stressful. Fighting alligators is no fun. Although administrators strive to cope as best they can, many are increasingly frustrated by the uncharted paths they follow and the sense of failure produced by endless crises. Responses to the perceived chaos and darkness of the swamp varies. Some managers "vote with their feet" and move on to new jobs. Many leave the public sector and take positions with private firms. Others rotate through the public service to positions in other jurisdictions. Some continue to do what they have done in the past with the hope that things soon will return to normal. Changes appear to them as anomalous, and they hope that as things return to normal, they will become more comfortable. They try to wait out change. Others take a positive attitude and try to alter the way they manage and the way their organizations operate. This adaptive behavior of the last group promises to assist them in learning to manage in the swampy conditions of contemporary society.

All of these types of responses are reasonable. Change of location and position often refreshes the manager; it is a cure for burnout and tedium. Past experience applied to new situations also often works. Incrementalism is useful, and, in the long run, some things do move toward historical norms which appear familiar. More active responses also succeed by opening the organization to more input from the environment and thereby enhancing learning on the part of administrators.

The New Public Administration of the 1960s stressed the idea of the *open system* which responds positively to change and to opportunities for change presented by a turbulent environment. (Marini 1971). A central theme was the desirability of bureaucrats and bureaucracies to learn from their environment and to strive purposefully to change institutional arrangements, rules, practices, and behavior to serve the public better. Much of the history of theory and practice of public administration since that time has been sorting out the principles and lessons of open systems as practitioners tried to live up to the lofty expectations and promises of the 1960s. Although some commentators feel that the New Public Administration and open systems approaches may not have changed public administration radically, such reforms as citizen involvement in bureaucracy, participatory management, program evaluation, and affirmative action have considerably altered and even improved the practice of public management in the United States (Waldo 1980; Mosher 1975).

AN ERA OF LIMITS

Many public managers no doubt reflect back to the earlier, Golden Age of public administration with considerable wishfulness. Even managers who matured in the 1960s and 1970s often speak of better, past times when government and bureaucracy were more positively viewed by the public and most administrators had high hopes and plentiful resources. Unfortunately, today is a time of major limits. Administrators often lack resources to do an adequate job of implementing policies and reaching specified goals. The public demands increasing amounts of services but frequently is not supportive. Elected officials are no less demanding than the public but often are much less supportive of the bureaucracy.

A host of recent changes presents the administrator with an

unpredictable environment, fewer resources, and a reduced menu of options. Among the most pressing changes are: (1) single interest politics, which increase demands upon the administrator for specific response to specific groups; (2) revitalization of conservatism, which constrains the resource base of governments and support for social welfare programs; and (3) slower economic growth, which reduces the resources available for use by public administrators.

Single Interest Politics

Public agencies as the principal participants in the policy processes are coming more and more to be the target of interest group activity. Interest groups typically have a narrow focus and strive toward getting administrators to do a specific thing a particular way for a target population. Historically, the narrow focus of these groups has been somewhat offset by the broader focus of political parties, legislative bodies, and bureaucracies. More and more candidates for and winners of public office at the state and local levels are *single interest candidates* (Prewitt 1970; Phillips 1982.) They run their campaigns, make their commitments, and work toward the achievement of narrowly defined, often self-interested goals such as reduction of the property tax, prohibition of abortion on demand, or abolishing the 55 mph speed limit. This narrow focus makes specific laws, court decisions, and agencies the likely target of their efforts.

Single interest politics diminishes the sense of community among citizens and reduces popular support for many social welfare and social justice programs. It puts public administrators in a severe bind. They have considerable incentive to narrow their focus and to cater to supporters from a few interest groups and selected elective officials. Their role in representation of third-party interests is diminished. As mentioned before, they have a tendency to develop clientele groups for support and to act as lobbyists in their own interest.

Fiscal and Political Conservatism

Many states and localities have adopted institutional constraints in the form of revenue, tax, or expenditure caps that limit the availability and use of tax funds. This reflects a growing tide of fiscal conservatism that retards the capacity of states and localities to fully use the potential tax base. Coupled with reduced funds from the national government through intergovernmental programs and transfers, this has greatly limited the amount of funds available to localities.

Neoconservatism goes beyond fiscal issues (Dolbeare 1984; Reich 1983). There is less support for social reform policies than there was fifteen to twenty years ago. It may be that real gains made in the recent past have convinced many people that we no longer need to give as much attention and public resources to housing, poverty, education, civil rights, and environmental programs as we did in the 1960s and 1970s. It also may be that failures of past social policies have made people suspicious of such efforts and agencies charged with their implementation. It probably is true that a history of waste and ineffectiveness in bureaucracy has convinced many Americans that government is not very efficient in dealing with social issues. Even liberals are much less optimistic about the capacity of governmental agencies to act. Whatever the roots, state, and especially local, bureaucracies must do their work in a much more critical, less supportive, and more conservative political environment (Lipset and Schneider 1983).

Slower Economic Growth

It is axiomatic that the United States now has an information- and service-based economy (Bluestone and Harrison, 1982). The fact that we lose more jobs annually than we produce in the industrial sector, that our industrial growth is very selective, that our agricultural, mining, and timber cutting activities are in decline, that we do not compete well internationally in many product and commodity markets, and that most of our real growth is in service, government, and communication sectors has profound effects on support for government activities. The Golden Age of public administration coincided with the period of our most profound national economic growth and dominance of many international markets. Even if we were not in a period of conservatism, the capacity of our regional and local economies to support government would be severely restricted. The rate of increase in the local and regional taxes is no longer as great as our appetite for services.

The consequences of these trends for public administrators are as contradictory as limiting. First, the resources available to public agencies, especially those at the state and local levels, are unlikely to increase at a rate commensurate with growth in the private sector and in the national public economy. Put another way, even if the national economy continues to prosper, local public sectors cannot capture much of that new growth as public revenues. Second, political conservatism and slower growth in the public sector have not retarded the demand for selected public services. Single interest politics and politicians increase rather than decrease the demand for specific governmental activities. A list of high-demand services includes increased police protection, more roads and highways, better outdoor recreational facilities, improved social security and services for the aged, safer domestic water supplies, more effective elementary and secondary schools, and expanded emergency medical services. Demands for more services come at the same time as pressure for more deregulation, streamlining of regulatory processes, less social welfare, and less government in general. Most localities face the problem of doing more with less in an uncongenial setting.

This decline in available resources has been coupled with an increased demand for excellence in the public service. This has put increased cross-pressures on public administrators. In the 1950s and 1960s, most public agencies became accustomed to growing budgets and much of the public administration literature seemed to be based upon an assumption of growth. The late 1970s and the 1980s witnessed a dramatic change in the assumption and brought new demands on public managers.

Under conditions of generous public budgets, it is taken for granted that as long as resources are expanding in an organization, things are easier to manage. Members of the organization can be given increased resources or at least are not likely to lose any of their resources. Subunits thus can be provided incentives to work together and accept guidance from the management of the organization. During times of decline in resources, however, the incentives are not there, and many stresses develop internally and externally (Levine 1978, 1979; Rubin 1985; Waldo 1980).

Public administrators have to deal with other bureaucrats, employee organizations (unions), clientele, the general public, and political leaders who all expect the same or higher levels of service even though the resources to provide service are diminished. Even if it is possible to convince these various interested parties that service levels have to be cut, establishing priorities is extremely difficult. Each actor tends to believe that the others should absorb the cut.

In social service agencies, cuts are especially difficult because resource cuts often mean that more people end up needing services. As fallout from other programs and employment losses mount, social service agencies are likely to see more clientele. With fewer resources, they are less able to serve those clientele, and frustration mounts for all concerned.

Within the organization, Levine (1979) argues that cutback management increases conflict among members of the organization and is detrimental to efforts to democratize organizational management. He also suggests that it reduces innovative and creative initiatives in organizations. Clearly, as fewer resources are available to managers, there are fewer for them to give their members. People are less likely to accept change and to work together when they are uncertain about their own security and the maintenance of their organization's viability. The challenge to managers is immense.

In addition to the practical implementation of cutbacks, managers have to deal with the psychology of it. Most societal pressures and management traditions equate growth with success and progress. Decline in resources and organizational size requires a new perspective. Not all managers are able to adjust to the new direction or assumptions.

SOME POSITIVE TRENDS

Not all change is confining. Some recent trends present public administrators with opportunities. Among the most promising are: (1) increased numbers of women and minorities in public life; (2) broader diffusion of humanistic management practices; and (3) widespread use of microcomputers by managers in the public sector. Managers and agencies need to seek out the positive side of these and other trends in order to maximize their capacity to perform in a socially and professionally credible manner in the face of an ever-changing environment.

Women and Minorities in Public Life

Increased numbers of minorities and women are running for office and being elected. Larger numbers of the same populations are entering the public service. This is a positive trend that offers considerable opportunity for improved public management. The absolute number of such candidates and officeholders is small, but the rate at which the numbers of women and minorities gain public office is increasing. Even if many are single interest candidates, they are expanding the range of values within which the bureaucracy operates. Any trend that increases rather than reduces the variety of values expressed in governmental arenas is a gain.

Likewise, changes in the numbers of women and minorities in the public service has made it more representative of the whole society (Cayer and Sigelman 1980; Dometrius 1984; Dometrius and Sigelman 1984; Eribes, Karnig, Cayer, and Welch 1984; Grabosky and Rosenbloom 1975; Huckle 1983). In some jurisdictions, the increases at the entry and middle levels are impressive (Sigelman and Cayer 1986). Mobility to the higher levels, especially for women, has not kept pace with increases at the entry level, but the increase in the relative numbers of women and minorities in many jurisdictions is changing the mix of public service employees (Sigelman and Cayer 1986; Huckle 1983; Dometrius 1984; Bayes 1985).

The impacts of these changes are potential and speculative at this time. A good argument can be made that such changes are opening up bureaucracies and infusing alternative ways of seeing and doing things. While some people see such changes as destabilizing and producing conflict, in the long run, they are likely to produce a more democratic governmental system and a less rigid, closed bureaucracy.

Humanistic and Democratic Management

One of the lasting contributions of the past three decades of management theory and practice has been the shift away from power-oriented practices, which stress dominance of top-level managers over their employees, toward those that empower lower-level employees (Bennis 1969; Garson and Overman 1983; Mintzberg 1979). More and more attention is given to the involvement of individual employees and groups of employees in the overall management of organizations. One cannot argue that fully participatory management has arrived or even that most public administrators buy into forms of participatory management. It is clear, however, that public administration practice is moving more toward a human relations, humanly expressive form of management. The new generation of public administrators seem to have strong commitment to humanistic approaches to management.

Diffusion and Use of Microcomputer Technology

The computer revolution has taken firm root in public administration. As previously mentioned, much of the impact of mainframe computers and electronic data processing was negative and dehumanizing. A kind of mystique developed around the application of computers to management. A computer elite came to dominate the development and use of large computers in public agencies. Access to and use of computers was retarded by poor training, cliques of knowledgeable users, and poor equipment. Many times, the adoption of a computer system appeared to the uninitiated administrator as a waste of resources that made the overall job of management more difficult.

While there is a residual of negative feelings about computers and resentment toward computer elites in many agencies, the infusion of microcomputers into everyday life has made the computer one of the most used tools in the office. The micro, personal computer and the wide variety of software for it have dispelled much of the mistrust and mystique surrounding computers. Much of the use of microcomputers is for word processing, but more and more managers use micro, mini, mainframe computers and computer networks for data management, communication, planning, time management, problem solving, and production control activities. Few technologies, except perhaps the telephone and copy machines, have had and are having such impacts upon how people and organizations work. Such impacts as reduced time in record keeping and management, more effective communication, and substitution of computer networks and electronic bulletin boards for face-to-face conversation were expected and have happened.

Less obvious has been the democratization of the workplace through the use of microcomputers. The radical decentralization of data sets and the access to data brought about by microcomputers poses many security and quality control issues, but it has freed individual workers from some of the negative constraints of hierarchy. Freedom of access to and use of information in an organization is a key part of democratization of administration. The microcomputer has made this literally possible, much to the chagrin of the mainframe elite.

RISK AND UNCERTAINTY

The net impact of the changes as outlined above probably cannot ever be known. Further, the precise impacts on a given agency in a given community are likely to be so specific as to defy much generalization. Finally, the response of the individual bureaucrat and bureaucracy also will alter the impacts such changes can and will have. Such changes produce different responses. The more creative the anticipation and response, the better chance that the net impacts will be positive or at least tolerable. Anticipation of change and positive response to it is one of the secrets of survival in the swamp.

Capacity To Handle Change

Lindblom (1959) suggested many years ago that our culture is best at "muddling through." That is, organizations have goals but no clear set of optional ways of achieving them, and because of living in the swamp, they tend to move incrementally toward approximate achievement of near substitutes for the originally defined goals. It is not an exaggeration to say that organizations seldom hit the intended target, but they sometimes come tolerably close. Equally often, we do not even come close. The more swampy the setting and the more elusive the goals, the harder it is to pursue plans that when implemented will reach the expected goals. Unfortunately, the planning and resource allocation effort itself takes place in swampy conditions.

Dealing with Risk and Uncertainty

How can we have any sense of order in the swamp? By trying to account for the unknown. Systems analysis usually recognizes three general states of environmental conditions: certainty, risk, and uncertainty.

Certainty is not much of a problem. If we know with certainty what will happen, it is fairly easy to select the correct option, allocate the appropriate level of resources, and achieve our goals with some clarity and surety. Most managers do confront such conditions, usually dealing with routine activities, which they assign or delegate to someone else.

The real tests of management are those circumstances in which the future is less well known and in which the most appropriate choice is not clear. This is where managers earn their salaries.

Risk is the condition under which the manager can estimate the occurrence of events. Under risk situations, there are two kinds of events: choices of ways of reaching goals and varying situational conditions that may affect the outcomes of a given alternative. An example will help show how the choices may be affected by different situational conditions. Suppose an elementary school principal is planning class assignments for the upcoming year and wants to know how many teachers to assign to third-grade classes. The choice is to assign one, two, or more teachers to teach third-grade students. The principal does not know, however, the precise number of third-grade students who will enroll in the upcoming year or the exact amount of funds available to hire supplementary teachers. The choice of how many teachers to assign is risky.

Under conditions of risk, the principal and school planners try to *estimate* the situational conditions. They try to guess the most likely number of students and level of additional funding available so as to allocate teachers accordingly. If their estimates are good, they will be able to make a plan that has a reasonable chance of success. Some managers and their staffs, trained in probability theory and operations research, make use of sophisticated quantitative methods to estimate the risks involved in their choices. Such techniques aid decision makers in estimating the possible impacts of situational conditions upon the usefulness of various alternative choices. The use of these techniques depends heavily upon the capacity to estimate the probability of any situational condition

taking place and the assignment of an estimated risk to each potential outcome. These techniques are used in such divergent activities
as meal planning in large hospitals and siting decisions for nuclear
reactors.

Many management situations involve estimation of risk. Management experience and training equip persons to handle true risk
situations. We have posited, however, that the manager lives in
the swamp where it is even difficult to estimate the probabilities of
occurrence of key events. Here managers face *uncertainty*, wherein
situational conditions can be reasonably assumed to be random.

Warren Bennis (1969), both a practicing manager and an academic, has characterized these uncertain management conditions
as the metaphor of the arrow. See Figure 6.1.

The arrow represents the organization moving through time
and space toward a target. Note that in our representation the
arrow is not about to hit the target. Good managers will attempt to
shift the movement of the arrow more toward the target but will
have limited success. Why is this so?

First, the target is probably elusive. Initially, it may have been
poorly defined and dimly perceived. Further, in a dynamic world
filled with changing expectations it may have moved.

Second, the main body of the arrow, which represents the living
organization, has momentum of its own. Most of the movement of

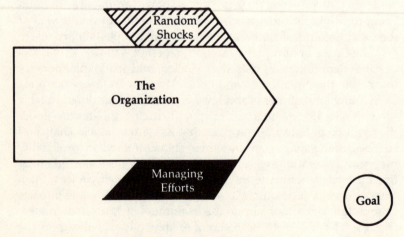

FIGURE 6.1: Arrow Metaphor

the arrow through time and space is the result of hundreds of thousands, perhaps millions, of decisions made by the scores of individuals who comprise the organization. These decisions, which range from such mundane concerns as "Will I go to work today" to such cosmic concerns as "There is a 6 percent shortfall in state revenue this year; where will I cut back," combine to push the arrow through space under its own momentum, not really under the control of anyone.

The bottom ear of the arrow, shaded in dark gray, represents the efforts of the managers to manage. They are trying to push the arrow more toward a path that will cause it to come closer to the target (which may be moving). Note that the mass of the ear is much, much smaller than the mass of the organization as a whole. This recognizes the fact that only a portion of the total work of the organization guides it to *direct* achievement of the formal goals of the unit.

The top ear, shaded in lighter gray, represents random, external shocks to the organization which also alter its path. Note that as illustrated the mass of this ear is much less than the mass of the main body but may vary in size under different circumstances. The external events are frequently as important as the constructive efforts of administrators in determining motion toward goals.

Since the shocks are random, some push it more toward the target and others away. The problem is that at any given moment at any given place in the journey toward or away from the target, managers are hard pressed to know just which shocks will affect the organization and in what direction they will push it.

FACING UP TO THE SWAMP

Management is an interesting but chancy game. The organization tends to go its own way. Managers try to anticipate helpful events and take advantage of them and to predict deleterious events and counter them. At the same time they do this, they attempt to adjust the internal practices and behavior of their organization to overcome inertia and enhance organizational capacity to handle negative shocks.

Responding in the Organization: More Efficient Management

Nearly every agency and manager will say they can do a better job if they have more resources. Given resource constraints, the issue becomes one of being more effective with fewer resources. Meeting resource reduction often is called *cutback management* (Levine 1978 and 1979). The main strategy in cutback efforts is to decide which past activities are least essential to the agency's mission and reducing or eliminating these until expenditures equal available resources.

Under severe resource reduction, this kind of response may be the best approach. Most agencies, however, do not fully use the resources they have. A more enlightened response to resource reduction is to take the opportunity to reform things internally. There are at least four different things that may be done.

The first is a variation of the general cutback strategy. It requires administrators to make sure that as much as possible of what the agency currently does leads to attainment of its mission and goals. Over time, many administrators get sloppy in their resource allocation and performance assessment activities. Resources often are devoted to activities that do not directly support agency goals. Managers periodically need to do an internal inventory and performance audit to see if all activities are necessary and if they can be done in a more effective manner. Few managers will fail to find activities to cut or reduce or change when conducting these serious kinds of self-evaluations.

A second approach is to improve the information available at various decision points. Lazy, content organizations make nearly all decisions according to some fixed routine. This is disastrous under tight resource conditions or in the face of a changing environment. More productive organizations strive to make sure there is considerable variety to the information available. This usually involves a wide cross section of the agency's employees in the gathering, management, interpretation and use of information. Such information-rich organizations most often make use of some kind of multilevel, participatory planning and management. Few public bureaucracies practice participatory management, but those few that do are advantaged by tapping into the information and knowledge base of all employees.

A third option is increased internal training. This sounds

counterintuitive because training is often treated as a frill and one of the first things cut in budget rollbacks. Yet many employees do not understand their role in and contribution to the overall organization. Many lack appropriate skills for the position they currently fill. Many also do not have commitment to and support for the goals of the organization. Training, which in the short run takes time and resources away from mainline, production activities, actually can save resources by making individual employees and work groups more effective. The problem is planning to reserve some resources for these activities even under resource constraints.

A final example, drawn from military organizations and defense contractors is the establishment of mobile teams of "troubleshooters" which are available to be sent to different places in the organization to put out "fires," lend special support, or temporarily increase resources available for a given task. This is difficult to accomplish under resource constraint conditions, but every organization under stress needs a small number of personnel in a team that has good cohesion and that can respond to many of the special tasks of the organization. This mobile team can be called upon by regular work units for special assistance and move from assignment to assignment to help make sure that key tasks are done on time.

In the Community: Developing Support and Contributions

Bureaucracies in the ordinary course of events are good at developing support systems for their lobbying activities with the legislature, executive, and other agencies. Frequently, they are very effective in developing strong relationships with clientele groups even to the detriment of the executive's attempts to control them. The same instincts and techniques may be used to enhance their capacity to respond positively to change.

Few bureaucracies make effective use of advisory boards and citizen groups. Yet they need a more broadly based information system and public support system to do well in the face of a rapidly changing environment (Needleman and Needleman 1974; Yin and Yates 1974). Some agencies, mostly among local governments, have learned that they can educate the public, develop broader positive support and enhance public acceptance and compliance with what they are trying to do by reaching out into the community and discussing things with ordinary citizens. This is called management by walking the feet. Managers and middle managers need to get out of their offices and meet with leaders and ordinary citizens in their native habitat. Regular solicitation of formal and informal input by private citizens and citizen organizations will provide administrators with valuable information concerning the performance of their agencies.

In addition to providing information or participating in decision making, in some instances ordinary citizens are regularly involved in the production and delivery of public services by agencies. This has been termed "coproduction" because citizens actually are part of the street-level bureaucracy in the sense that they join with the public bureaucracy in providing, producing, and delivering the service (Bish and Neubert 1977; Wilson 1982; Rich 1981). In several municipal-type services such as police protection, recreation, education, and libraries, direct citizen involvement in the "production stream" of agencies has resulted in improved services, reduced costs, and greater understanding and support for the bureaucracy. In fact, coproduction has proven so effective that it is often a preferred option when localities face possible reduction in revenues.

Coproduction activities may take many forms. A few examples will illustrate the variety of contributions citizens may make to the production of services. A common example is some effort made by citizens to expand, extend, or supplement the public service, such as a "Neighborhood Watch" in which local residents form cooperative arrangements to watch over the property of the neighbors and to report any suspicious activities to the local police authorities. Another example is the voluntary teachers or teachers' aides who, without compensation, assist regular teachers in special math or reading sessions. This is a particularly interesting example since it puts underused community resources to public use. A last example is the suicide hotline, which melds private and public resources into a communication center to which depressed and potentially suicidal persons may call for help. Every city and town has hundreds to thousands of such examples of coproduction. What is new is that agencies under fiscal stress are seeking out new and expanded opportunities to secure direct private and voluntary contributions to bureaucratic production of services.

These efforts to involve bureaucracies more in community affairs and citizens more in production of services has beneficial effects exceeding cost reduction and improvement of services. They provide more joint understanding and more public support. They tend to reduce both public hostility toward government and bureaucratic cynicism toward the public. There are, however, some things about coproduction about which we need to be cautious. An important issue is the extent to which public services come to be privately provided. As bureaucracies become more and more dependent upon the contributions of given groups or clusters of citizens, the relative array and distribution of services is apt to be skewed. Those who play most tend to determine the game. Another consideration is the extent to which those service sectors that receive ready private or voluntary support are denied relative support from public budgets. There is some balance point, but it would be grossly unfair and inequitable to reduce a given service commitment, primarily because supplementary services were available. Finally, the line between public and private may become blurred. The public mission of the public agency may become diminished and the redistributive goals of some services such as education may be lost. Serious conflicts of interest may develop as public agencies depend more and more upon resources and efforts of selective groups. The more the public service has a social welfare function, the more likely that these three concerns become important equity issues.

Efforts by practicing administrators to improve the capacity of themselves, their staffs, and their organizations to live in the swamp will work. In the long run, however, public administration as a profession needs to give continued attention to the education of new generations of managers. It will be future members of the profession, well educated and trained in progressive management theories and methods who will ensure continued excellence in the public service in a turbulent environment.

IMPROVING PUBLIC ADMINISTRATION EDUCATION

One of the secrets of the success of the reformers of the first half of this century in promoting the public service was the fostering of the development of an administrative class. This was both good and bad. It produced a dedicated group of well-trained professionals. Some of the negative aspects of the growing administrative elite are well known (McConnell 1966; Lowi 1979; Thayer 1981). For a long time, especially in the upper-middle and top echelons, the administrative class has been very homogeneous, a white, male, upper-middle-class bastion. It has used its expertise and special languages to close itself off from the rest of society. It has been a brake against the liberal and conservative reforms and kept many policies from being completely implemented. Some of the positive accomplishments of this class of administrators are less well acknowledged, but in historical perspective, are very important. Overwhelmingly, the American public service is honest and without corruption. The very expertise that has made it arrogant and closed also has permitted remarkable achievements especially in applied technology and social policy. And finally, much of the burden of humanizing big government has, ironically, been borne by bureaucrats as sort of a modern, late-twentieth-century noblesse oblige.

As pointed out in the earlier discussions of bureaucracy and organizational behavior, the report on the net value of bureaucracy and bureaucratic reform is incomplete. It is worth considering for a brief time some of the things that might be done to make the administrative class better at making bureaucracy more democratic and more effective through improved education and training of administrators.

Affirmative action has had a mixed history and limited successes (Bayes 1985; Bonaparth 1982; Cayer and Schaefer 1981; Thompson and Browne, 1978). A key problem is that the pool of women and minorities and handicapped, the so-called protected classes, is woefully small given the demand for persons from these groups. A good strategy for improving affirmative action and for improving the public service in general would be a more concerted effort to improve the pool by accelerated education and training of members of the protected classes. There has been some improvement in the numbers of handicapped, minorities, and women getting terminal degrees in management and public administration, but not enough to make much of a difference. Likewise, training and cross-training inside of agencies and jurisdictions has provided a better pool and some mobility for members of protected classes but not sufficient to change the gender mix, social demographics, or racial distribution of the administrative class very much.

The National Association of Schools of Public Administration and Affairs (NASPAA) and the American Society for Public Administration (ASPA) take a firm stand on affirmative action and provide guidelines, materials, and workshops aimed at improving affirmative action practices as well as expanding the pool of members of the protected classes. The burden, however, rests with the several-hundred undergraduate and graduate programs of public administration and business in the United States. Until they are able to attract, recruit, retain, and graduate large numbers of women, minorities, and handicapped there will be little improvement in the pool available to carry out affirmative action.

A related issue is change in the curriculum for education for public management. Both NASPAA and ASPA have been increasingly active in pushing for a consistent, rigorous curricula especially for the Master of Public Administration, which is becoming the nominal terminal degree in the field. Under the leadership of several deans of schools of public administration, public policy, and public affairs, as well as from activists in educational reform, affirmative action groups and others, public administration has begun to change its curriculum on a national basis. NASPAA was recently approved as a national accrediting body for public administration. What has been peer review will become formal accreditation. The peer review system formerly used by NASPAA did much to bring many public administration master's programs into compliance with national standards.

There is controversy over the standards adopted by NASPAA, the validity of the approval process, and the effectiveness of the review program that began in 1978. Nonetheless, the NASPAA standards suggest that the New Public Administration of the 1960s and the 1970s is bearing fruit. NASPAA curriculum guidelines try to balance skill development with a broader appreciation of the history of the field, a philosophic understanding of management, and a positive view of the public service.

Much has been done recently to bring public administration into closer harmony with its turbulent environment. It remains, however, a stressed profession and a rapidly changing field of study. The swamp is not getting any easier to manage. Crisis management often is the order of the day. In the next chapter, the idea of a "new and improved" public administration is explored. Public administration and public administrators must be able to make hard choices and to provide moral leadership in a time when public regard for the public service has waned.

REFERENCES

Bayes, Jane H. 1985. "Women in Public Administration in the United States, Upward Mobility and Career Advancement." Paper presented at the XIIIth World Congress of the International Political Science Association, Paris, July 15–20.

Bennis, Warren G. 1969. *Organizational Development: Its Nature, Origins, and Prospects.* Menlo Park, Calif.: Addison-Wesley.

Bish, Frances P., and Nancy M. Neubert. 1977. "Citizen Contributions to the Production of Community Safety and Security." In *Financing Local Government: New Approaches to Old Problems,* ed. M. S. Rosentraub, 34–50. Ft. Collins, Colo.: Western Social Science Association.

Bluestone, Barry, and Bennett Harrison. 1982. *The Deindustrialization of America.* New York: Basic Books.

Bonaparth, Ellen. 1982. *Women, Power and Policy.* N.Y.: Pergamon.

Cayer, N. Joseph, and Roger C. Schaefer. 1981. "Affirmative Action and Municipal Employees." *Social Science Quarterly,* 62: 487–494.

Cayer, N. Joseph, and Lee Sigelman. 1980. "Minorities and Women in State and Local Government: 1973–1975." *Public Administration Review,* 40 (September/October): 443–450.

Dolbeare, Kenneth M. 1984. *The Politics of Economic Renewal.* Chatham, N.J.: Chatham House.

Dometrius, N. C. 1984. "Minorities and Women Among State Agency Leaders." *Social Science Quarterly,* 65:127–137.

Dometrius, N. C., and L. Sigelman. 1984. "Assessing Progress Toward Affirmative Action Goals in State and Local Government: A New Benchmark." *Public Administration Review,* 44: 241–246.

Eribes, R. A., A. K. Karnig, N. J. Cayer, and S. Welch. 1984. "Women in Municipal Bureaucracies." Paper presented at the Annual Western Political Science Conference, Sacramento, Calif. (April 12–14).

Garson, G. David, and E. S. Overman. 1983. *Public Management Research in the United States.* New York: Praeger.

Grabosky, P., and D. Rosenbloom. 1975. "Racial and Ethnic Integration in the Federal Service." *Social Science Quarterly,* 56 (June): 71–84.

Huckle, P. 1983. "A Decade's Difference: Mid-Level Managers and Affirmative Action." *Public Personnel Management,* 12: 249–257.

Levine, Charles H. 1978. "Organizational Decline and Cutback Management." *Public Administration Review,* 38: 316–325.

Levine, Charles H. 1979. "More on Cutback Management: Hard Questions for Hard Times," *Public Administration Review,* 39: 179–189.

Lindblom, Charles E. 1959. "The Science of Muddling Through." *Public Administration Review,* 19: 79–88.

Lipset, Seymour Martin, and William Schneider. 1983. *The Confidence Gap: Business, Labor and Government in the Public Mind.* New York: Free Press.

Lowi, Theodore. 1979. *The End of Liberalism*. 2d ed. New York: Norton.

Marini, Frank, ed. 1971. *Toward a New Public Administration: The Minnowbrook Perspective*. Scranton, Pa.: Chandler.

McConnell, Grant. 1966. *Private Power and American Democracy*. New York: Knopf.

Mintzberg, Henry. 1979. *The Structuring of Organizations*. Engelwood Cliffs, N.J.: Prentice-Hall.

Mosher, Frederick, ed. 1975. *American Public Administration: Past, Present, Future*. University, Ala.: University of Alabama Press.

Needleman, Martin L., and Carolyn Emerson Needleman. 1974. *Guerrillas in the Bureaucracy*. New York: Wiley.

Phillips, Kevin, 1982. *Post-Conservation America*. New York: Random House.

Prewitt, Kenneth. 1970. "Political Ambitions, Volunteerism, and Electoral Accountability." *American Political Science Review*, 64: 5–17.

Reich, Robert B. 1983. *The Next American Frontier*. New York: Times Books.

Rich, Richard C. 1981. "Interaction of the Voluntary and Governmental Sectors: Toward an Understanding of the Coproduction of Municipal Services." *Administration and Society*, 13: 59–76.

Rubin, Irene S. 1985. *Shirking the Federal Government*. New York: Longman.

Sigelman, Lee, and N. Joseph Cayer. 1986. "Minorities, Women, and Public Sector Jobs: A Status Report." In *Affirmative Action: Theory, Analysis, and Prospects*, eds. Michael W. Coombs and John Gruhl, 91–111. Jefferson, N.C.: McFarland and Company.

Thayer, Frederick C. 1981. *An End To Hierarchy and Competition*. New York: Franklin Watts.

Thompson, Frank J., and Bonnie Browne. 1978. "Commitment to the Disadvantaged Among Urban Administrators: The Case of Minority Hiring." *Urban Affairs Quarterly*, 13: 355–378.

Waldo, Dwight, 1980. *The Enterprise of Public Administration*. Novato, Calif.: Chandler.

Wilson, Kirk K. 1982. "Citizen Coproduction as a Mode of Participation: Conjectures and Models." *Journal of Urban Affairs*, 3: 37–50.

Yin, Robert K., and Douglas Yates. 1974. *Street Level Government: Assessing Decentralization and Urban Services*. Santa Monica, Calif.: Rand Corporation.

Chapter 7

A NEW AND IMPROVED PUBLIC ADMINISTRATION

As this book has demonstrated, public administration in the United States is characterized by tensions among numerous competing values. There is no reason to believe that the future will be any different. Social change and increasing complexity of social organization are certain to remain parts of the relevant environment and dynamic of public organization. While the specific issues are likely to vary from time to time, it is also likely that the fundamental issues identified in this text will continue to be at the root of adaptation of public administration to social reality.

AN INTEGRATED APPROACH TO PUBLIC ADMINISTRATION

Large organizations are a fact of life in our complex society. The efforts to organize government activities along bureaucratic lines assumed a need for rational approaches to accomplishing tasks. This rationality often stressed quantitative methods and empirical evidence at the expense of more qualitative concerns. Over time, a conflict developed between values associated with bureaucratic rationality and qualitative values such as social justice, quality of life, participation, creativity, and innovation. These qualitative values attained high levels of visibility and importance in the post–World War II era, especially since the 1960s. Bureaucratic traditions and organizations often seemed at odds with these new values.

Even some of the concerns of the traditionalists would seem to be at odds with the values of our democratic society. For example, accountability and responsiveness have always been major issues in public administration, but many of the features of rational bureaucracy work against responsiveness to democratic impulses. Rational bureaucracy is supposed to foster efficiency, but political democracy, especially as practiced under the United States Constitution, builds in high political costs and inefficiencies (Karl 1987). Checks and balances were created in our government to assure that no one person or part of government could exercise effective centralized control over the whole. Although American bureaucracy long has valued efficiency, values other than efficiency are extremely important to democratic polities. The emergence of social equity and the other concerns associated with the Civil Rights Movement of the 1960s are examples of political democracy that might and do get in the way of bureaucratic efficiency.

Many students of public affairs during the 1960s seemed to focus on responsiveness as the primary value that should guide all government activity. As a general principle, people favor responsive government. So long as political leaders who support their views are in power, they seem to want the bureaucracy to be responsive. When, however, someone representing the opposite ideological stance attains a leadership position, the same idealists may want bureaucracy to be less responsive and actually become obstructionist in its approach to the new political leadership (Price 1975). For example, social activists of the 1960s and 1970s generally do not want the current bureaucracy to be responsive to the Reagan administration although bureaucratic responsiveness was one of their major concerns earlier. Of course, supporters of Reagan administration perspectives also want a responsive bureaucracy—and are likely to change perspectives should a new administration represent strongly different ideological positions. Thus, the fervor with which one wants organizations to respond is determined, in part, by whether one's interests are likely to be served.

As Sirianni (1984) and Gulick (1987) note, there is never likely to be a perfect solution to the problems of organizations in a complex society, nor can organizations solve all social problems. Many organization theorists spent their time attempting to develop a model to solve virtually all organizational problems. As students of organization theory are well aware, such approaches led to a large body of literature pointing out the inadequacies of each of the proffered models. Sirianni correctly suggests that organization theory needs to accept the pluralism of modern society as a given and recognize its need for organization theory to accommodate many alternatives. Each situation or problem is likely to call for something different in organization approaches. Recognizing that fact can lead to efforts at developing alternative organization theories to meet the need. Obviously, there is still need for some stability and parameters, but flexibility and adaptability are important components in producing relevant organizations.

The tendency of organizations to emphasize particular norms to the exclusion of others is a major problem in constraining their adaptability. Bureaucracies go to great lengths to mute dissent or opposition when they would be more prudent in encouraging such activity (Weinstein 1979). Dissent and opposition to prevailing norms, within limits, can enhance the vitality and relevance of organizations.

ON THE STREETS: MAKING POLICY CONSUMABLE

President Truman was famous for a sign on his desk. It said: "THE BUCK STOPS HERE." That sign is an object lesson about life at the top. What about life at the other end of the hierarchy? Michael Parenti (1974), among others, has argued that the final point of discretion is at the street level. The teacher, the police officer, the lifeguard, the social worker, the person at the reserve desk of the library, and millions of others are the final deliverers of goods and services. They are the last decision makers in the long chain of providers from policy recommendation through implementation.

In a very practical, and often final sense, these holders of the lowest-level, service production-oriented jobs give meaning to public policy. Despite popular images of an unresponsive bureaucracy, the street-level bureaucrat usually is sensitive to the needs of the consumer of public goods and services and mediates against the sharp edges of rules meant to ensure a legal, rational order. Conversely, the street-level bureaucrat also often is the last blank face and rule-bound decision maker in a long sequence of unfeeling responses to human needs.

The problem for democratic society is the trade-off between the pursuit of organizational, bureaucratic, and consumer needs. One may visualize the citizen-consumer as the last person bearing the costs of the bureaucratic state. For example, consider the older citizen who has specific health care, nutritional, and recreational needs and lacks personal means to pay fully for privately provided services. Many communities use both public and private resources to provide special programs and facilities for the elderly. Meals-on-wheels, senior citizen centers, discount fares on buses, and health clinics for the elderly are common attempts to provide special care and services for older members of the community. Such efforts may effectively reduce the "consumption" costs that the elderly bear in their use of publicly provided services. The monetary, transportation, and psychological costs associated with consumption of normally distributed services are lowered for this sector of the population.

Making public services more consumable for the community in general and for specific target populations has been a goal for American public policy and public administration for decades. Many of the experimental programs of the 1960s and 1970s were attempts to repackage and redeliver public services to enhance their usefulness. There is a serious practical problem with reduction of consumption costs. Usually such efforts raise the average production costs of services. Both the producing agencies and the taxpayers must bear additional increments to reduce consumption costs. In many cases there is an inverse relationship between reducing the costs borne by the final consumer and the costs borne by the producing unit and jurisdiction.

Bilingual education programs may be used as an example to illustrate the inverse relationship between production and consumption costs. The recruitment and training of special teachers, the development, printing, and distribution of specialized curriculum and materials, and the injection of bilingual programs into traditional classrooms all increased the costs of education. The efforts to meet the particular needs of a special, non-English-speaking population raised the average cost of providing education in many local school districts. At the same time, it made the education offered to special populations more usable and more consumable. The non-English-speaking students were able to make better use of the educational service provided.

If under fiscal stress and changes in federal and state laws, local school districts cut back bilingual programs to save money, the production costs of education may be reduced. There is likely to be a corresponding rise in the costs borne by the non-English-speaking students. No longer will their development of English language skills be fostered through special programs. Instead, individual students and their families will be expected to pick up the psychological and material costs of learning English in the regular classroom setting or outside the schools. The personal acquisition of language skills becomes relatively more expensive for these special populations. In the long run, the reduction of bilingual education will result in citizens lacking skills in English and having fewer opportunities for social development and advancement.

Although bilingual education is a special case, it illustrates a general point: efforts to reduce consumption costs often result in additional production costs. Conversely, decreases in production costs often carry with them increases in consumption costs. For example, red tape is the inverse of lowering consumption costs. Long lines, time delays, centralized delivery systems, special forms, rules and procedures, jargon, rigid legal constraints, and even large scale, tend to raise the costs borne by the citizen consumer. In the normal world of bureaucracy, more attention is given to production costs and less attention to consumption costs.

In a time of cutback management and reduced public support for many services, the prospect of pricing many service consumers out of the publicly provided services systems is great. Recreation and fire services are timely examples. Both of these services are amenable to "user fees" in which potential users are asked to pay some out-of-pocket cost (in addition to the general taxes supporting the jurisdiction) to make use of such facilities as tennis courts, swimming pools, and basketball courts or to pay a special charge for fire-protection services. Although in most cases such user fees are nominal, in many cases they are not, and effectively raise the cost of services beyond the reach of poorer citizens. Efforts to economize through contracting, higher user fees, increased dependence on private market producers, and economies of large-scale production systems will effectively shift more and more of the actual costs of public services to the individual consumers.

The dilemma of bureaucratic behavior becomes the extent to which middle- and lower-level members of the hierarchy can and will "subsidize" less fortunate clients or the extent to which transactions are such that more and more costs are passed on. The final arbiter of social justice is the last person who can increase or reduce consumption costs.

THE LIMITS OF THE WELFARE STATE AND LIBERAL MARKET ECONOMY

The social assistance programs of the 1960s such as Headstart, Community Action Programs, and the Job Corps extended the welfare state. As we saw in chapters 2 and 6, the resurgence of fiscal and political conservatism has pushed the social programs of the 1960s and 1970s back. Currently, there is considerable debate about the actual effectiveness and lasting impacts of the social welfare policies, market control mechanisms, and environmental regulations of the past several decades. Some commentators suggest that the liberal policies of the New Deal, Fair Deal, Great Society, and New Federalism have been less than successful. Some even feel that the continued problems of widespread poverty, poor health, high levels of crime, inadequate housing, and unstable regional economies are the result of failed welfare and regulatory policies. Others argue that we have done too little and that we are in a period of regression brought about by cutbacks in governmental efforts. They fear that we will lose any gains made in income redistribution, improved opportunities for education, and environmental quality.

Part of the argument is ideological and simply shows that there are still strong conservative and liberal perspectives and factions in the United States. Part of the concern transcends political perspective and partisanship. On the one hand, our policy tenaciously clings to the idea of individualism, privatism, and a free market. On the other hand, our nation is dependent upon the rules, regulations, activities, and services of the welfare and regulatory state. This contradiction presents a philosophical and practical bind. People want a community composed of individuals cooperatively working together, but lack the basic perspective and institutions to do this easily. Citizens thrive on the products of the welfare and regulatory state but push to reduce the size and impact of public institutions.

The bureaucrat is indeed in the middle. The special role, competence, and power of the bureaucrat and bureaucracy suggest that if this contradiction can be solved, it will be solved by an even more enlightened and humane public service. Institutional and procedural reforms over the years have tried to balance individualism and community values. Such reforms as open meeting laws, requirements for citizen participation, affirmative action programs, and equal opportunity requirements have adjusted the modern American state to new issues and crises. Yet, as suggested in the earlier discussion of organizations and organizational behavior, such reforms are marginal and only partially complete.

The hard facts and hard choices are such that we have to admit that the use of public power, like that of private power, cannot solve all problems. There are "wicked problems" (Harmon and Mayer 1986) which by definition are not easy to solve or cannot be solved at all. Crime is an example of a public problem that is wicked in more ways than one. Crime is wicked in the ordinary sense of the word. It is bad because it hurts people. It also is wicked because it is not clear how to prevent and control crime. Crime increases despite all our efforts to reduce it. At the present, there is no rational solution to the problem of crime in our society.

There are large-scale problems which can only be partially solved because the causes and the external effects are so hard to manage. Air pollution is such a problem. Most of the causes or sources of typical urban air pollution are known. It is, however, a classic case of a problem fraught with externalities. It is hard to put a boundary around air pollution and prescribe a rational solution to it. Most air quality control strategies—testing of automobiles, inspection of coal- and gas-burning facilities, regulation of the use of toxic materials, and conservation of fuels—only handle portions of the production of pollution. Even in coastal Southern California, which has perhaps the most complete air pollution control program in the nation, only parts of the problem can be handled. When dealing with smog, people have had to learn to live with partial solutions. There are hard choices and trade-offs. Nearly all efforts to focus on a problem or set of problems shift public resources from other problems. Thus, the menu may be large, but the options are limited.

The Golden Age of public administration is over. In that Golden Age, agencies often had sufficient resources to attempt many solutions to many problems. Most governmental jurisdictions no longer have sufficient slack resources to invest in a wide menu of issues. At least at the local level, this lesson is being driven home forcefully. Reductions in funds available from the national government, state and locally imposed taxing and spending limits, and weakened state economies all have reduced the amount of public funds available to localities. Many communities actively explore ways to reduce public services, make more use of private market providers, and engage in joint ventures with private sector entrepreneurs. Traditional lines between public and private sectors are becoming blurred as municipal governments move more toward shared risk, investment, production, delivery, and income from new development and redevelopment with private vendors.

The "newest" new public administration may well result from the efforts of localities to adjust to limits: fiscal, institutional, and political. Local governments often lack the tax base or authority to tax effectively the local economy. Coupled with reductions in funds available from the state and national governments, they are fiscally squeezed. Institutional limits such as constraints on the ability to annex growing suburbs to established cities or to engage in joint private-public undertakings weaken the capacity of local governments to adjust to changing conditions. Political limits include unstable coalitions of interest groups and fiscal conservatism. Taken together, these limiting factors place local and state officials in a new world of public administration. In this new world of limits, administrators struggle to carry out much of the welfare state without adequate resources. This adjustment often is wholly pragmatic, unconscious, and not well thought out. Nonetheless, the role and the function of public administration is being reshaped as managers try to overcome the considerable problems of administering the welfare and regulatory state in a post-liberal time.

SOME "NEW" CONTROVERSIES FOR PUBLIC ADMINISTRATION

The past twenty-five years have been years of great change for public administration, indeed for society as a whole. Many of the social movements have had very direct impact on public administration. In particular, the societal emphasis on issues of social justice and quality of life have created new demands and expectations for public administrators. No longer are they evaluated by how efficient they are in their activities, but also in terms of how their activities contribute to the values of social justice and quality of life. The more traditional concerns of efficiency and responsiveness are still concerns, but now public bureaucracy is expected to respond to those concerns as well as the new ones.

In reality, the new concerns are extensions or different interpretations of the fundamental issues public administrators have always been expected to consider. In dealing with social justice and quality of life issues, public administrators are responding to public interests and concerns. In addition to being responsive to democratic society's values, dealing with these issues also represents some of the basic issues addressed by traditional bureaucracy. The concepts of neutrality and impersonality really presume a sense of equity in treatment. The advocates of social justice are asking that bureaucracy provide equal opportunity for all sectors of society to participate. Thus, their demands are partially consistent with the precepts of bureaucratic rationality. In the views of those supporting social equity issues, bureaucracy has always responded to those interests that have the most resources; it is now being asked to respond without reference to the interest's resources, or to even the balance by showing preference for those who otherwise do not have the resources to participate.

There is yet another way in which the concerns of contemporary bureaucracy can be viewed as a continuation of more traditional issues in public administration. The processes of administration receive much attention in analyses of public administration. While there were efforts to eliminate the political from the administrative aspects of public affairs in the early development of public administration, it has never been possible to separate the two completely. What has become evident in contemporary public administration is that political processes are important to the administrative process. Those interests that are successful in gaining the attention of public bureaucracy are those that have access. They use their political resources to affect what is going on and use bargaining processes to gain support for their interests.

It is commonplace to speak of the influence of specialized interests and single issue interest groups. These political actors participate in the political process at large, but they also concentrate a lot of attention on the public bureaucracy. The influence such groups have on bureaucracies is significant for the ability of our political system to integrate the varied interests into some form of public interest. If access and influence are too great for narrow interests, the general public may see its interests given short shrift. Implications for legitimacy of public institutions and confidence in the political system are immense.

Newfound emphasis on ethics and moral foundations of bureaucratic behavior also have antecedents in the past. The moral fervor of the reformers of the nineteenth century and the early twentieth century was clear. During the period in which Scientific Management and managerial efficiency held public administration's greatest attention, the moral and ethical issues were less visible, but they were always a part of the assumptions on which good management was based.

During the 1970s, however, ethical behavior of public managers again became a major issue. Public confidence in public institutions eroded and the Nixon administration's Watergate scandal focused attention on the personal behavior of public servants (Bowman 1981). Scandals within the Reagan administration during the 1980s have kept the issue of ethics on the public agenda. While the administration speaks of the need for restoring a high moral fabric to American politics and public life, its deeds have left people confused. Lapses in judgment among many administration officials in the relationship of official and personal business, and outright misleading of the public on some major issues, have raised questions. Possible violation of law by the highest levels of the administration in the Iran arms deals only add to the cynicism people have about the ethics of public officials.

Ethics will continue to be an issue of importance to public administration. There is not likely to be any resolution of the argument as to whether ethical behavior can best be assured through reliance on the character and professionalism of the individual bureaucrat (Friedrich 1940) or through attempts to regulate behavior through legislation and rules and regulations (Finer 1941). Certainly both approaches are used in the United States, but there is a strong tendency to try to insure against any kind of abuse by developing a prohibition against it. The dilemma is that detailed prohibitions may make it difficult for the bureaucrat to act creatively and innovatively. Creative and innovative approaches to problems and jobs may be more valuable to the political system than avoiding abuse by specific rules. The question becomes one of whether the risk inherent in allowing widespread discretion is balanced by the potential for effective solutions to problems or delivery of service.

The issues to be addressed by public administration are the issues that face society. Despite the popularity of those advocating reduction of government intervention in our lives, it is unlikely that such change will occur. Instead, as new problems develop, government is likely to be asked to step in and solve them. We only hope that the fundamental issues of public administration discussed in this book will contribute to an understanding of how public administration can and is likely to respond. The capacity of bureaucracy to adjust to and embrace change will be important determinants of its effectiveness and ability to emerge from the swamp.

REFERENCES

Bowman, James S. 1981. "The Management of Ethics: Codes of Conduct in Organizations." *Public Personnel Management*, 10: 59–66.

Finer, Herman. 1941. "Administrative Responsibility in Democratic Government." *Public Administration Review*, 1: 335–350.

Friedrich, Carl J. 1940. "Public Policy and the Nature of Administrative Responsibility." *Public Policy*, 1: 3–24.

Gulick, Luther. 1987. "Time and Public Administration." *Public Administration Review*, 47: 115–119.

Harmon, Michael M., and Richard T. Mayer. 1986. *Organization Theory for Public Administration*. Boston: Little, Brown.

Karl, Barry D. 1987. "The American Bureaucrat: A History of Sheep in Wolves' Clothing." *Public Administration Review*, 47: 26–34.

Levine, Charles H. 1978. "Organizational Decline and Cutback Management." *Public Administration Review*, 38: 316–325.

Levine, Charles H. 1979. "More on Cutback Management: Hard Questions for Hard Times." *Public Administration Review*, 39: 179–183.

Parenti, Michael. 1974. *Democracy for the Few*. New York: St. Martin's Press.

Price, Don K. 1975. "1984 and Beyond: Social Engineering or Political Values." In *American Public Administration: Past, Present, and Future*, ed. Frederick C. Mosher, 233–252. University, Ala.: University of Alabama Press.

Rubin, Irene S. 1985. *Shrinking the Federal Government*. New York: Longman.

Sirianni, Carmen. 1984. "Participation, Opportunity, and Equality: Toward a Pluralist Organizational Model." In *Critical Studies in Organization and Bureaucracy*, eds. Frank Fischer and Carmen Sirianni, 482–503. Philadelphia: Temple University Press.

Waldo, Dwight. 1980. *The Enterprise of Public Administration*. Novato, Calif.: Chandler & Sharp.

Weinstein, Deena. 1979. *Bureaucratic Opposition: Challenging Abuses at the Workplace*. New York: Pergamon.

Index